W9-AKV-216

This Is
My Story
This Is
My Song.

A WIFE DISCOVERS
IT'S NEVER TOO LATE.

Copyright © 1994 by Frances Cardone.

All rights reserved.
Printed in the United States of America.
International Standard Book Number: 1-883928-05-2
Library of Congress Catalog Card Number: 94-075410

Scripture quotations unless otherwise noted are taken from
the King James Version.

Scripture quotations marked RSV are taken from the
Revised Standard Version of the Bible, Old Testament
Section, Copyright 1952; New Testament section, First
Edition, Copyright 1946; Second Edition © Copyright 1971
by Division of Christian Education of the National Council
of the Churches of Christ in the United States of America

Scripture quotations marked TLB are taken from The
Living Bible. Copyright © 1971 by Tyndale House
Publishers, Wheaton, Illinois 60187. All rights reserved.

Scripture quotations marked NKJV are taken from The
Holy Bible, New King James Version. Copyright © 1982 by
Thomas Nelson, Inc.

The song, Where the Roses Never Fade, used by permission
of the Benson Music Group, Inc. Copyright © 1942 by
Stamps-Baxter Music/MBI. All rights reserved.

Published by:
Longwood Communications
397 Kingslake Drive
DeBary, FL 32713
904–774–1991

To my husband, Michael, Sr. who lovingly taught me how to become the help mate God intended me to be — not only in business, but in life. I've been blessed because of you.

"Live happily with the husband you love through the fleeting days of life, for the husband God gives you is your best reward down here for all your earthly toil." (Ecclesiastes 9:9) (Paraphrased from the Living Bible).

And the days have been fleeting...just as my book was going to press, on October 19th, 1994, my dear husband left to be with his precious Lord after an extended illness. My grief is tempered by knowing that I will join him in our Savior's presence when God calls me home someday.

This Is My Story This Is My Song

Contents

This Is My Story This Is My Song

WHY DID I WRITE THIS BOOK?

I'm accustomed to writing things like recipes, letters and entries into accounting journals. But in no way would I have ever considered writing a book. Sure, my husband, Michael, wrote a book, *Never Too Late,* in which he told how God led him to start up a new company at the age of fifty-five.

But folks kept asking me: "Frances, how were *you* involved in all that?"

"How did you feel when others called your husband crazy for coming up with such a scheme when any sensible person would gladly take retirement?"

Others wanted to know how a person my age could go back to work to help run a company after raising a family. "Where did you find the energy? How did you keep going?"

And then there were those who wondered about

disagreements. One woman said, "My husband and I argue about which television channel to watch. How did you two get along on the thousand-and-one things it takes to run a business?"

To all of the questions, I had only one answer: Prayer and trust in God.

But that only led to a lot of other questions. "*How* do you find God's guidance? What happens when you don't get answers? How do you pray when terrible things happen?"

That's why I decided to write this book. It was a struggle. But if it will help others in their walk through life, it will be worth it.

I pray that my experience in facing problems and tragedies will help you through yours.

God bless you.

Frances Cardone

AN ENJOYABLE ENCOUNTER

Some years ago my husband was invited by the founder of a large manufacturing company in Philadelphia to speak to his employees. Usually I accompany him on these trips, but—to a factory?

However, since I believe one must sublimate negative feelings in favor of one's mate, I went along, although a bit grudgingly. But I was delighted I did.

We were given a tour of an unusual factory complex which is operated on godly precepts. That is why, I believe, Cardone Industries has grown from a small basement shop to the world's largest private remanufacturer of auto parts in just twenty-three years. But most enjoyable was meeting its founder, Michael Cardone, and his wife, Frances. The two started their business together when both were in their fifties. From the very beginning they dedicated themselves to Christian principles and, come what may—fires, financial crises, even earthquakes—they have never wavered from them.

As we talked with the Cardones, I was impressed by their mutually supportive relationship, which has withstood so many of the crises that sorely test a marriage: career change, devastating illnesses and, worst of all, the loss of a child.

Yet the two of them, now in their seventies, forge ahead with a positive attitude toward life. Frances and I had a good visit, and I learned much from her. This perky woman with bright, shining eyes had such good, common-sense ideas on family relationships and how to get along with a hard-driving husband that I suggested she write about her experiences.

Self-effacing, she shrank from the idea. "Oh, I couldn't do that," she winced. But I convinced her that if I could tell about my life with Norman in *Secrets of Staying in Love*, she certainly could write about helping her husband build and operate factories. And so she did. I'm sure you'll enjoy it.

Mrs. Norman Vincent Peale

Chapter One

THE EXECUTIVE WIFE

I will never forget that night. It had all started at dinner when my fifty-five-year-old husband, Michael, said he had something important to talk about.

"Sure, Mike," I said. I knew he was frustrated at work, and I sensed it was all going to come to a head soon. For some months he had been coming home from his office depressed. As we would say in Italian, he was *molte afflito.*

After we cleared away the dishes, we walked into our den. I sat down, picked up some dress material I was working on and smiled up at him. My instinct told me what was putting his nerves on edge. Mike was president of an auto-parts remanufacturing company.

He had started Cardo on nickels and dimes as a very young man, and it had become quite successful. In the meantime his four brothers had become partners in the business with him. However, within the past few years they had had some disagreements about company practices.

Like most men, Mike brought his anxieties home with him. And let me tell you this was not the most enjoyable time of my life.

Sometimes he'd be feeling so out of sorts that he would respond with a sharp remark. But I had learned to be an executive wife and would find something nice to say in reply. Then he would apologize, and we would have a nice evening.

If I had fired back at him, it would have been like throwing gasoline on a fire. Tempers would flare like Mount Vesuvius, and soon we might be saying things to each other we would later regret.

However, by now I had learned to practice what the Bible advises in Proverbs 15:1, "A soft answer turneth away wrath." I had finally learned to be an executive wife.

Is this someone who is part of a corporation? Yes, I believe a wife is a partner of the most important corporation in the world, the family. *Corporate* comes from the Latin word *corpus,* meaning body. And *corporate,* according to Webster's Dictionary, means "united into one body." If the wife is not a good executive, the body of the marriage—the family—is in danger of falling apart.

Families are disintegrating all over our country today. Records show that one out of two marriages end in divorce. And the strength of our nation rests on the stability of its families. Nowhere was this more emphasized than in the recent presidential election. All candidates talked of the importance of family values and what their administration would do to bolster them.

But government has little to do with strengthening family values. It is up to each individual husband and wife to follow the God-given principles for a strong family that have been laid down in Scripture.

I know I will get into trouble with some people for saying this, but I firmly believe the husband is the head of the house. If you don't believe this, look it up in the Bible. In 1 Corinthians 11:3, Paul writes: "But I want you to understand that the head of every man is Christ, the head of a woman is her husband, and the head of Christ is God" (RSV). I haven't seen it written any plainer. It's easy to see that God has given the husband the attributes for his responsibility. He is stronger, tougher, better suited to protect the family.

You have often heard of the Indian wife who obediently walks behind her husband on the trail. A friend of mine was talking to a real Indian chief in British Columbia about this.

"Of course the man should go ahead," said Chief Kitpou. "What if a bear attacks? The man is best equipped to fight it, to protect his wife, whom he loves."

By the same token, the man of the house should take the lead in consideration of the wife he loves.

Already I can hear the scream of some in the so-called women's liberation movement. "How dare you say such a thing! You are diminishing womanhood!"

"Honey," I say to this, "you've got it a little mixed

up. The man is the head, but the wife is his helpmate. They are partners, yes. But each has his or her own special job to do."

Some wise person put it beautifully:

The first woman was created from the rib of a man. She was not made from his head to top him, nor from his feet to be trampled upon by him, but out of his side to be equal to him, under his arm to be protected by him, and near his heart to be loved by him.

To this end, I believe God has given women special gifts of their own. An executive wife uses them to the fullest. Men have these gifts, too, of course. But I believe the women have a special edge in applying them to their families.

One of them is compassion, the ability to see another person's point of view. When a child is crying, the mother seeks the cause and tries to comfort the little one. When a husband is grumpy and irritable, an executive wife seeks the reason behind his mood and attempts to help him.

The key to all this is communication, keeping the lines of conversation open. Both husband and wife must feel completely free to share his or her most intimate concerns, needs and problems with the other. This includes gripes and irritations, whether it's something as petty as a husband not putting his dirty socks in the hamper, the wife not replacing the cap of the toothpaste tube, or something as major as a husband not giving enough time to his family, or a wife who runs up her family's credit card.

Little problems will not grow into big ones if they're

discussed early in open, frank communication. Without communication, a marriage is in trouble.

And so it was that November night in 1969 when Mike and I talked.

He sat down across from me, cleared his throat and said: "Fran, I feel it's time for me to leave Cardo and start something new."

My heart gave a little start. I looked at him intently, my needle poised in a stitch. His deciding to retire would not have surprised me. It was the "start something new" that jolted me. After all, we were in our middle fifties, and I had looked forward to Mike's retiring soon. I wanted to travel and do all the things we had looked forward to for years.

Moreover, I knew with Mike that "something new" would not be a part-time thing. When he threw himself into something, it was like the American invasion of Normandy on D-Day.

He got up from his chair and paced back and forth across the room. "It's going to cost us, Fran. We'll have to give up my salary, our medical coverage, life insurance, everything." He stopped and stared at me.

"If you feel differently about it, Fran," he said, "just say the word, and I'll forget it."

I leaned down and bit a thread to give myself time to think this through. My first reaction was to say that perhaps now was the time for him to take it easier. After all, he had been working hard ever since he was a little boy, delivering papers in his hometown of Hughestown in northeastern Pennsylvania. Our daughter, Ruth, was married and settled. Our son, Michael Jr., would soon be out of college and on his own.

Most people our age would think of winding down.

And, besides, whatever Mike started, I knew it would involve me in one way or another. That's just the way we worked, ever since I had helped him deliver rebuilt windshield wipers to customers back in our early days. Did I want to get back into the nitty gritty of the business world? I shuddered.

"Fran?"

I looked up at this husband God had given me, the man I had spent thirty-five years with, and breathed a little prayer of thanksgiving.

"Fran," he pressed, "I know it means giving up an awful lot. But if you feel differently in any way...."

I put down my sewing. "Look, Mike," I laughed. "I came naked into this world, and naked I'm going out. Of course I'm with you...all the way."

He gave a big sigh of relief and leaned down and kissed me. Twenty years seemed to drop off his shoulders.

That was the beginning of Cardone Industries, the auto parts remanufacturing firm Mike started a short time later. Yes, he did go into it like the Normandy invasion. And, yes, I was right there in the trenches working alongside him.

I know my husband would not have started his new enterprise if I was the least big backward about it. He would have taken his retirement, played a lot of golf and probably ended up the most bored man in Philadelphia. But I believe his knowing he had an executive wife who would back him up gave him the courage to go ahead.

In the twenty-three years since then, Cardone Industries has changed the lives of thousands of people and added a new dimension in remanufacturing to American business. And I feel a real part of it.

Communication is vital to every marriage, no matter what your husband does. He may be an accountant, a salesman, an auto mechanic or a school teacher. But thoughtful give-and-take between the two of you is his greatest help for success.

Why do married men live longer than single men? This has been proven time and again in national surveys. I believe it's because most married men have a helpmate who is *there* to offer encouragement, sympathy and compassion. She is there to help him over the rough spots and, yes, to give him the kind of advice that only a woman can offer.

Of course, to me, a deep reliance on prayer and guidance from the Lord are indispensable. Without them, I don't believe Cardone Industries would exist today. Prayer has been a vital part of my life since I can remember. In fact, my mother says it started when I was an infant.

It all began when Mama asked God for a sign.

This Is My Story This Is My Song

Chapter Two

MAMA MIA!

It happened in a little apartment in South Philadelphia. Mama and Papa had come to America separately from a little town in Italy called Troia. It's so small you probably can't find it on a map, but it is near Foggia. Each of them had stepped off the boat with nothing but two suitcases and a dream. Their dream was to offer a good life to the children each hoped to have. The dream took shape after they met in the United States and were married.

They were only in this country a year when I was born, their first child. However, when I was two months old, Mama became very sick. She had a chronic digestive tract problem and suffered so much that she and Papa decided there was only one thing to do: pack up and return to Troia, where Mama's mother would take care of her. It was a wrenching decision. Not the least of their worries was the ocean trip. Coming over, their ship had tossed and rolled so much in terrible storms. After that I think Mama didn't even want to look at a *picture* of the ocean.

If they had gone back to Italy, I'm sure my parents never would have returned to America. So for a while it looked as if I would grow up in Italy, live under Mussolini, suffer the war and, well, who knows *what* would have happened?

Enter Mrs. Ianelli, a relative. This good-hearted woman had come to visit Mama and look over her new *bambino*. They had small talk; Mama served her biscotti and coffee. Then Mrs. Ianelli got down to business.

"Jennie, I feel so bad that you are leaving and are not yet saved. Think of that long trip ahead and what might happen on it." She put her hand on Mama's shoulder. "Please, Jennie, why don't you accept Jesus Christ as your Lord and Savior?"

Mama wasn't sure about this. After all, she went to church regularly, she lit candles and she prayed. But accepting Jesus? She had never considered Him a real Person with whom she could have a relationship, and, well, it all sounded so…so different.

She thought for a bit, taking a bit of cannoli. Finally she put her coffee cup down and said: "All right, but the only way I'll accept the Lord is if He gives me a sign."

People in Mama's generation often looked for signs. After all, if a sign was good enough for Gideon, it was good enough for them. However, in this case I'm pretty sure it was simply Mama's way of putting Mrs. Ianelli off.

It was quiet in that little kitchen as Mrs. Ianelli waited, wondering, I'm sure, if she should simply give up and say her good-byes. Mama told me later she hoped her relative would do just that. After all, Mama had a big tub of laundry waiting for her attention. Papa was a waiter, and he always had to have clean white shirts.

The clock on the wall ticked loudly in the silence. Finally, Mama turned and looked at the bedroom where I lay sleeping my crib. She said: "Let me see if my baby is all right." This time, she thought, Mrs. Ianelli would be sure to leave.

Mama got up, walked into the bedroom and cried out in astonishment. The relative rushed in, and the two stood staring at me in awe.

The baby was fine. However, as she lay on her back sound asleep, her little hands were clasped together as if in prayer. *It was the sign.*

The two women stared at each other. Mama crossed herself. Then, her face pale, she turned to Mrs. Ianelli and said humbly, "Yes, I am ready to accept Jesus."

They knelt together right in that bedroom, and Mrs. Ianelli prayed for Mama to receive Jesus Christ into her life. Mama confessed and repented of her sins, believed Jesus had provided her salvation, accepted God's forgiveness and told Mrs. Ianelli along with God, Jesus and any angels that were listening that Jesus was the Lord of her life.

Then something far more astonishing than a baby praying happened in that room. Mama was healed of her ailment, right then and there.

The Lizzis, of course, remained in the United States. And every time I sing *The Star Spangled Banner* and watch the American flag go by in a parade, I give thanks in my heart for Mrs. Ianelli's stubbornness.

Was I, a two-month-old baby, praying? It might well have been so. For I believe our little ones are so fresh from heaven the world hasn't touched them yet. I often think of the old story about why we have that little cleft above our lips. They say an angel put it there; just before we leave heaven as a new baby, an angel presses his finger to our lips and says: "Shhhhh, do not tell them heaven's secrets down there."

Then again, it may have just been gas pains.

Whatever it was, I do know for sure that the Lord used it to get my mother into heaven. And she found heaven on earth too. That was when Mama and Papa joined *La Chiesa Italiano Pentecostale.*

Because of *La Chiesa,* I had a joy-filled life growing up.

Was our family wealthy?

Absolutely not. Papa was a waiter who worked long hours for very little. Sometimes the restaurant he'd be working in would close, and he'd walk the streets looking for a job. Mama had to make do with very little. There were times she pinched the pennies so hard I thought I could hear Abraham Lincoln yell, "Ouch!"

It was the church around the corner from our house that made the difference. Besides being a place where we could worship God exuberantly with music, it was our family community center. In our little church it was one for all and all for one. Everybody was one big family. And in those days families had lots of children.

Mama didn't bite her nails worrying when she learned a new baby was coming; she trusted God would take care of us. And so my four brothers, two of them twins, and sister arrived in regular succession.

So you can see our church had an abundance of children. And that meant I had lots of friends I could laugh, talk and play with. For a shy child like me, it was a place where I felt accepted. That gave me courage to come out of myself, to focus attention on the other person.

Oh, how many sad people I know who grew up in wealthy homes. Children who had everything given to them. They swam and played tennis at country clubs, were sent to exclusive schools and summer camps. And yet, so many of them became entrapped in drugs and alcohol.

Every child wants to feel secure, and that means being accepted by their peers. Too often privileged children, shunted aside by parents, find their schools a combat field of outdoing one another, of survival. And so often in vying for acceptance, they accept drugs and alcohol to be in the *in* crowd.

In every Bible-believing church I know of today, the young people have the security of knowing they are *in* with Jesus Christ. They do not need the false security of their peers' acceptance. In our church, knowing we all shared the same Jesus gave us the unabashed freedom of relating honestly and happily with each other as equals.

I learned this truth early, and it gave me great freedom. When you look up at Jesus, you find you don't look down on anybody. By the same token, you *know* that nobody can look *down* on you. Everyone is equal at the foot of the cross. This one realization has given me freedom to mix freely and confidently with government leaders, corporate executives and celebrities. It has given me the freedom to be relaxed with people whom society may consider inferior, whether they be homeless or street people. No matter what the world may try to tell us, we are all the same in the eyes of Jesus.

That's why in our church we all had so much fun together. But not until I was thirteen did I find out how wonderful life could be. That's when I went forward with others to the altar, knelt and accepted Christ as the Lord of my life. Afterward, we all celebrated at my house.

The kids called our place the "Red Cross Station," because they always got refreshed and refilled there. Before evening services, I would go to Hanscoms Bakery and buy a tray of day-old coffee cakes and doughnuts for 15 cents. Just before the others came streaming into the house, I'd heat the tray in the oven under a damp cloth and make hot cocoa. Then we'd sing all the old songs together.

Wouldn't this world be a better place if we could have just a little of that today? Our home should be a place of peace and happiness. For my father it was a retreat. When Papa would come home from work late at night after a hard day in the restaurant, Mama would help him take off his old tuxedo, which is what waiters wore in those days, and have a cup of hot coffee ready for him. The contented look on his face as he sipped the coffee and she rubbed his shoulders was an unforgettable picture of domestic tranquility. Mama made sure Papa knew he was the most important person in her life. As a result, he never stopped at the corner saloon for a pick-me-up, to talk with the boys or shoot pool to "relax." He couldn't wait to get home.

I was reminded of this recently when a young wife came to me to complain tearfully about her husband not coming home on time. "He says he has to work late at the office," she cried. "And then I find he visits a singles bar."

I had to ask: "What is a singles bar?"

When she told me it is a place where young people go to meet each other, I asked her, "What are you like when he gets home?"

"Oh," she said, wiping her eyes, "I'm usually tired and out of sorts. After all, I've also put in a hard day at work." I understood for after our children were grown, I had also put in my time working during our marriage. But I had to tell her: "Look, it doesn't take much to put on a fresh face and greet him with a smile when he walks in. Ask him what kind of day he had. If he says it was terrible, be sympathetic; let him know how important he is to you."

A few months later this same young woman came to me looking like a new person. "You know, Mrs. Cardone, I realized I wasn't the kind of person *I* would like to meet on coming home," she said. "So I took your advice, and even had his favorite dish on the stove. Our life hasn't been the same since.

"But soon I will have to quit my job and stay home," she added.

"How come?" I asked, happy that she was able to do this.

She gave me a funny smile. "Because I'm pregnant."

I was so glad I hugged her. I realize that of many young couples today, both have to work to make ends meet. But if there is any way they can make do on less, it is better for both husband and wife if he is the breadwinner and she makes a home. Often this will take sacrifices—not buying that second car, foregoing Caribbean cruises or staying clear of fancy restaurants. But let me tell you, I've had experience both ways. The sacrifice it takes is well worth it.

Watching my mother make a home is what convinced me of this. And as I think of how much I learned by just watching her, it convinces me that the old adage is true: "It's not what you *say* but what you *do* that counts."

This was brought home to me one summer morning when I was about eleven years old, scrubbing diapers on the back porch in a big galvanized metal tub. This was one of my regular jobs, the privilege of being a first-born you might say. Only I wasn't so thrilled about the privilege. Every time I thought I'd be saying good-bye to my last tub of diapers, Mama would be expecting again.

On this summer morning I was busy scrubbing, wet dark curls plastered to my perspiring forehead. I stopped to take the big tan bar of Fels Naptha soap and with a knife cut some slivers for the tub water. At this moment I heard the screen door open, and there stood Mama with an awed expression on her face. "You do that just like I do, and I never taught you," she said.

But of course she taught me. I watched Mama all the time and did everything she did. That is the way children learn, by seeing what their elders do.

That is why we must be so careful. I remember the old saying, part of which goes:

If a child lives with kindness, he will be kind.

If he lives with love, he will be loving.

If he lives with fairness, he will be fair.

A father once told me how he learned this lesson. It happened on a snowy winter day. The snow was deep, and as he carefully stepped through it on his way to the garage, he heard small grunts behind him. He turned to see his four-year-old son placing his little feet into his father's footprints. "I'm following you, Daddy," cried the little tyke. The father said to me: "You know, I never realized how careful a parent must be. He is a walking role model for his kids."

Of course, I learned more from Mama than how to cut pieces off a bar of soap. She was an indefatigable church worker. I do not mean she was running the women's circle or baking cakes, which is what "church work" seems to mean to a lot of women today. I mean she worked for the Lord. She brought more people to the Lord than even Mrs. Ianelli.

If someone wasn't in church that day, Mama was on the phone. "Whatsammater, Mrs. Rinaldi, I didn't see you today. We were afraid you were sick."

If Mrs. Rinaldi was indisposed, then Mama and some of the other ladies would be right over with food. Whatever kept Mrs. Rinaldi away, one thing was for sure: She felt *wanted.* Ask anyone today; there's no better feeling in the world than knowing you are needed.

One of the saddest statistics I have seen lately is that, on a national average, 80 percent of people in nursing homes have no visitors. Isn't that terrible? You can be sure there was no one in *La Chiesa Italiano Pentecostale* who ever felt that way.

In fact, when I would go with Mama to visit a sick person, I'd see her peek into their icebox. "Mama," I asked, "why do you do this?"

She looked down at me through serious brown eyes and put a hand on my shoulder. "Francee, I look to see if they have enough food to eat. Sometimes they are too proud to admit they don't."

In our church I never knew anyone to go hungry.

Another lesson Mama taught me by example: how to bring people to church. *Bring* is the key word. Usually when you invite someone to church, he or she will smile politely and say, "Yes, I'll come sometime!" Of course, they often don't because most people are a little embarrassed about going to a new place by themselves. When Mama invited people, she would add: "And I'll come by your house and pick you up." When shown this kind of interest, the person would very likely go. And once they discovered how great it was, they would come on their own after that.

However, once Mama got a big scare because of her witnessing. She had spent a long time with Mrs. Contani one winter telling how the Lord would help her. Mrs. Contani had ten children, and even at my young age I felt sorry for her.

Finally, Mrs. Contani accepted the Lord. What a wonderful baptismal service it was! Our church had a big tank for baptizing. Our pastor would baptize new believers in the name of the Father, the Son and the Holy Spirit.

Mrs. Contani rose out of the water looking so happy.

She hardly got dried off and dressed when, praising the Lord loudly, she rushed out of the church to go home to her children.

Late that night I was awakened by the sound of Mama pacing around her room in her nightgown. Rubbing sleep from my eyes, I asked: "Mama, what is wrong?"

"Oh," she sighed, clasping her hand to her forehead. "I've been worrying all night. After a cold-water baptism, Mrs. Contani had a 15-block walk home. It's winter time! Oh, dear God," Mama cried, "don't let her get pneumonia. Her ten children need her."

Next morning she couldn't wait to call Mrs. Contani. Her hand trembled as she picked up the phone. I held my breath, afraid of how Mama would take it if Mrs. Contani even had the sniffles.

"Hello...Mrs. Contani?"

The big smile spreading across Mama's face told me everything. She hung up the phone and danced around the room. "Praise the Lord!" exclaimed Mama, "Mrs. Contani says she never felt better in her life!"

Mama was convinced, and I believe it too. When we do something that glorifies God, somehow we are protected.

But I have to say Papa didn't feel that way when he came home from the auction that day.

This Is My Story This Is My Song

Chapter Three

MUSIC! MUSIC! MUSIC!

S ome men watch baseball, others play cards. Papa
liked to go to auctions. In those days little
auctions were held everywhere. The post office
would sell off unclaimed articles. Salvage companies
would put up merchandise retrieved from train wrecks,
fires and bankruptcies. Papa would go to auctions
mostly for the entertainment. With what little money he
had, he was probably outbid on everything he tried for.
Sure, maybe he would come home proudly bearing a set
of salt and pepper shakers, or a framed print. Mama
didn't mind his little fun. She figured he had very little
entertainment in life. And the little bit of money he
spent wasn't missed. Sure, she could have used the
money he spent in a year for a new dress, which she

hardly ever had. But Mama well knew the give-and-take principle of marriage. That is why they got along so well.

But sparks flew on the day he came home from one particular auction. By then we had moved from the apartment to a row house in South Philadelphia, and I was in the kitchen scrubbing diapers as usual. I heard Papa call: "Francee, O Francee." I could tell he was excited. Drying my hands, I rushed into the living room. There he stood, brown eyes glowing, holding something out to me. It was a violin!

By some miracle he had come up with the winning bid for it.

"Francee," he said, "I'm going to teach you how to play it."

I was thrilled but thought his promise a bit strange. I never knew Papa could play the violin, or any other instrument for that matter. Then Mama came into the room holding one of my new little twin brothers, whom she had just changed.

"What?" she cried, "You bring a zuzu into the house, and I have five little ones to raise! Don't you know Francee is the only one I got to help me? And you want her to spend her time with..." She was so upset she couldn't finish her sentence.

Papa calmed her. "No, no *cara mia*, only a little time each day she play."

"Mama, I promise," I squealed. "I will help you just as much as before!" Grumbling, she left the room, my baby brother on her hip. I picked up the beautiful instrument, a thrill flooding me. I had always felt God had given me a gift for music, but until now I never had the opportunity to put it to use. As I admired the violin's mellow glow and savored the aroma of its polished maple and spruce, I knew I would learn to play it. I did not know then it would change my life later in a very important way.

Of course, Papa couldn't teach me. "Francee," he said when I asked about learning, "when I come home from work I'm so tired." But he was true to his word. He paid a man in our church to teach me for twenty-five cents a lesson. Not until later did I find out he had given up his auction fun to help his little girl exercise her talent.

Each night when he'd come home he would sit down, lean back in his chair and say: "Francee, play me something."

Even at the squeaks and squalls of my early beginnings, a big smile would cross his face, and he'd sigh. "Oh, Francee that is *so* beautiful!"

Perhaps Papa knew what he was doing by complimenting me. Or maybe it was the instinct of a good father. But where he could have easily winced in agony and asked me to play on the back porch, he made me feel like a virtuoso. As a result, I practiced harder and harder to the point where people started asking me to play for them. And though Mama pretended to grumble about the time I devoted to music, I know she was secretly proud of me. For it was she who told our pastor I was ready to play at services.

As much as I enjoyed the violin, there was one instrument I dreamed of someday playing even more: the piano. But for us to own one? It was as impossible as Papa being able to buy his own restaurant. These were Depression days.

However, I enjoyed the next best thing: hearing an accomplished artist play the piano. We were very fortunate to have Mr. and Mrs. Capuzzi live next door to us. Both were concert pianists. And every day they would practice on their Steinway piano. Oh, what beautiful music. As the melodious notes drifted into our yard, I would lean my head against the fence in ecstasy, savoring each chord.

Our pastor taught us that we should always tell God what was in our hearts. But could I talk to God about something as worldly as a piano? I mustered up enough nerve to talk to our pastor about it. "Frances, we can talk to God about anything beautiful," he answered. "He has given His children the gift of music. Look," he said, opening his ever-present Bible. "Here, right in 1 Chronicles 15:16, (RSV) 'David also commanded the chiefs of the Levites to appoint their brethren as the singers who should play loudly on musical instruments, on harps and lyres and cymbals, to raise sounds of joy.'" He closed his Bible and patted my head: "No, my child, it is not wrong to tell Him whatever is on your heart."

And so I did: "Please, Father God," I prayed, "I would love to play the piano. So if You see fit for me to do so, please in the name of Jesus, help it come about."

By now, whenever the notes from Capuzzi's piano could be heard, Mama knew where to find me—standing at the back fence, lost in reverie. She would shake her head and say, "That child is such a dreamer."

The Capuzzios also noticed my interest. Gracious people, they would talk to me as they sat on their porch.

"We understand you like to hear us play," said Mrs.

Capuzzi. She was a heavy-set woman with long black hair which she wore piled on top of her head when she and her husband left for an evening's performance. Now, in the afternoon, she let it flow down behind her like a raven-black waterfall. But it was her eyes which I remember, soft and lustrous. So I didn't feel bashful at all when she spoke. "Oh yes," I said. "I just love to hear you both play the piano. I wish I could play, but...." I stared down at my worn, scuffed shoes, still moist from washing diapers. I did not have to say anything more. The Capuzzis knew a family with five children and a father who waited on tables had no money for a piano.

I saw them look at each other. Mr. Capuzzi put his long slender fingers together beneath his chin as if he were deep in thought. The afternoon sun glinted off his silver hair. Then he nodded to his wife.

Mrs. Capuzzi said: "Come up here and sit down with us, Frances." I couldn't understand what she had in mind, but thrilled to be so honored, I sprang up onto their porch. Too nervous to sit down, I backed against a porch post, twisting the hem of my gingham dress.

Mr. Capuzzi cleared his throat. "You know, tomorrow we are getting a new piano. Until now we did not know what to do with our old one. It has been like our child. We didn't want to sell it or give it to anybody because we didn't know whether or not they would appreciate it." He put his hand on his wife's knee and looked at her.

"Would *you* like to have it Frances?" she asked. "We know you'd appreciate it."

Flustered, I groped for words. "Oh, Mrs. Capuzzi, no, I couldn't. We...we don't have the money."

"But we want to *give* it to you, Frances," she said, leaning forward and taking my hand. "We know you would appreciate it."

I still couldn't believe it. My head was spinning.

"But...but we have no money," I stuttered.

Mrs. Capuzzi gently took my chin in her soft hand and raised my face to hers. "*Cara bambina,* please understand. We are *giving* it to you."

The back porch seemed to tremble and the sun dance. Hardly believing what I had heard, I backed up and almost fell down the steps.

"Our new piano is being delivered tomorrow," continued Mrs. Capuzzi, "and we'll have the men bring your piano over to your house."

Almost in a trance, I turned and groped to find my way home. I couldn't even tell Mama, I was so stunned. It was a dream, and I was afraid to wake up from it.

The next afternoon our doorbell rang. Mama put my little brother down, wiped her hands with a towel, sighed and went to the door. I peeked from around the kitchen door. She opened the front door. Two huge burly men stood there, a piano behind them. I stood frozen in unbelief and ecstasy.

"We have a piano for you, lady," said one of the men.

Mama turned red, then white. "He did it again!" she cried. By this time I had edged up behind her.

"First he buys a violin, now it's a piano!"

I tried to tell Mama; my mouth worked, but no words came out.

Finally, in resignation, Mama pointed to the living-room corner. "Bring it in," she sighed, "what can I do?

I have a husband who thinks he is Mr. Rockefeller."

Grunting and puffing, the men rolled the piano through the door and into the living room, where it stood in regal splendor. I couldn't believe it. We had a piano!

After the men left, Mama went to change one of my little brothers who was wailing loudly. As she changed his diaper, I started to tell her where the piano came from. But she exclaimed, a safety pin in her mouth, "He did it again! I got a houseful of kids, and *he* goes out and buys a piano!" She pulled the safety pin from her mouth and fastened the diaper. "We don't need a piano. I need somebody to help me with the kids!"

Finally, I worked up the courage. "But, Mama, Papa didn't buy that piano."

She wheeled and faced me, outrage on her face. "Whatta you mean, you saying you and him got together and *you* asked him to buy that piano?" Fearing she was about to strike me, I backed away.

"No, uh—"

"Now you tell me the truth!"

"But, Mama..."

She slumped in a chair, sighing and shaking her head. "I don't know what I'm gonna do...I don't know what I'm gonna do."

At last I blurted: "Mama, the Capuzzis *gave* us the piano."

She looked at me in amazement, rose from her chair and advanced on me. "Where do you get these ideas, Francesca?" When Mama used my full name in Italian, I knew I was in deep trouble.

"If you don't believe me," I sniffled, "put on your

hat and coat and go ask them."

Mama stared at me a moment, then, shaking her head, she put on her coat and marched out of the house. I'm sure she believed her oldest daughter had lost her mind.

Five minutes later she returned with shocked unbelief written over her face. She hung up her coat and slumped down in a chair. "I'm sorry, *bambina*," she sighed. "I just couldn't believe it. Those people…those good people to do a thing like that for us?"

I didn't tell Mama I had been praying for a piano. Nor had I told the Lord I wanted a Steinway. But I was beginning to learn God does not do anything halfway.

I also didn't know this piano would be one of God's ways to lead me to the man I would marry.

Chapter Four

THE BOYFRIEND

For a week the beautiful piano stood there. But I couldn't touch it. Mama had locked it. She knew that once I began fingering those keys, I would be entrapped. And then who would help her with the children? "Maybe later," Mama said, carefully locking the keyboard and putting the key in her purse. "After I don't need so much help with the house."

I was crestfallen. Then I got an idea.

"Mama, you haven't been able to go to evening services because of the children. Why don't you go and let me babysit?" By now I was old enough to take this responsibility.

Mama thought for a minute, then brightened. "Oh, Francee, you really mean it?" She looked out the window wistfully. "I haven't been to evening church in so long."

After supper, I cleared the table and started washing dishes. "You go, Mama, I'll take care of things."

After she left, I quickly finished the dishes and straightened up the house. Then I got a long, thin scissors out of Mama's sewing box, took it to the piano and carefully worked the lock. Someone way back in my ancestry must have been a locksmith, for I was able to work that scissors' blade just so. *Voila!* The piano was unlocked.

I heard a little gasp behind me. I turned to see my young brothers and sister watching me, their eyes wide as pizza pans. *Uh-oh,* I thought, *now Mama will be sure to find out.* My mind raced.

"Kids," I said, "how would you like me to make some candy for you?"

"Yeah! Yeah!" They jumped up and down in excitement.

"But on one condition," I said.

They sat very quiet. I could see I had them in the palm of my hand.

"You don't tell Mama I played the piano, I make the candy."

"Yes, yes," they screamed. "We promise! We promise!"

I went to the kitchen, put some cocoa and sugar on the stove and started making fudge. While waiting for it to cool, I went to the piano.

From my violin playing I knew what to do with my right hand, but I had no idea what to do with my left. I did know it worked the bass. Even so, as I experimented, it was wonderful as my fingers ran up and down the ivories. I found I could even come up with some familiar tunes.

But what about the bass? As I sat puzzling, I heard the key going in the front door, and I quickly closed the piano lid; it made a little click as it locked. I went to the door to meet Mama.

As she walked into the house, she looked around and exclaimed, "Oh, Francee, you've made me so happy. Church was just wonderful. And look here. I come home to find a clean, sparkling house and..." she walked into the kitchen. "And the happy children. Why, look, you've made fudge for them."

She leaned down and kissed me. "Francee, you're the most obedient little girl."

The next day I went over to the Capuzzis. They showed me how to use my left hand for the bass and how to work the foot pedals. Because I was so eager to learn, I understood quickly.

Mama went to evening services every week after that. And every week I would practice on the piano. Of course, I would straighten up the house and take care of my brothers and sister first. Mother couldn't believe how happy the kids were and said I was becoming the best candy maker in Philadelphia.

Finally, after some months, I was learning to play fairly well. Even my brothers and sister would come into the living room to listen, the greatest test of all. And then one day I faced my moment of truth.

Mama was busy ironing in the kitchen. It was a hot day, and perspiration beaded her forehead as she worked on Papa's shirts. I stole into the living room and with the scissors quietly opened the piano, sat down and started playing the melody of "What a Friend We Have in Jesus."

It was Mama's favorite hymn.

The pounding of the iron stopped. I kept on playing softly, and then I heard a sigh from the doorway. Mama was standing there enthralled, watching me. "Francee," she said, her voice husky with emotion. "It's beautiful! Wherever did you learn to play like that?"

I jumped up from the piano, ran over to her and, with tears streaming down my face, put my arms around her and confessed everything.

From then on Mama found the money for me to take piano lessons. Papa loved hearing me play so much he learned to play the violin, and we both "played loudly on musical instruments...to raise sounds of joy."

By the time I was seventeen, sounds of another type began to be heard in our house—voices of young men interested more in Frances Lizzi than the cocoa we served.

Now don't get me wrong; these were not boys coming to take me out on a date. Heaven forbid! In our circle, a young lady did not go out with a boy without a chaperone—usually her brother. This may seem quaint and old-fashioned today, but in many ways it had it all over the "hang loose" dating game today. In the first place, a young man did not take these get-togethers lightly. He was usually fairly serious about his intentions before embarking on such an event, which usually included paying for the brother's soda at the ice-cream parlor where such dates usually ended up. With a chaperone along, any intimacy was confined to discussions about one's goals and philosophy of life.

What better way for two people to know each other? I believe if we had more of this kind of dating today, there would be a lot fewer divorces. Young people would really get to know each other, which is the foundation for a sound marriage.

Fun? I know of few things more exciting and fulfilling than a spirited conversation. When I see the bored expressions on the faces of so many young couples today, I am convinced that the mental stimulation of our day far outweighed the physical stimulation of today.

Much of our conversation centered around our ambitions. I made it very clear that I wanted to be a pastor's wife. I was so impressed by our church's pastor and the wonderful work he did, I could think of no better calling in life than to be a helpmate to such a man.

In no way did this forestall any suitor's intentions. I think they all felt they would be able to change my mind. But I was very positive about my goal.

Then along came a young man who made me think twice. I shall call him Sal. Handsome, with curly black hair and dark flashing eyes, I found him intriguing. My oldest brother, who chaperoned us, liked him too.

However, Mama with the intuition of most women, had doubts. One night as I was preparing to go out with Sal, she came into the bedroom and sat on the bed.

"You like this young man?"

"Oh, yes, Mama," I said, brushing my hair.

She picked up my dress from the bed, studied a seam in it and said quietly: "I don't think he's for you, Francee."

I turned, hairbrush frozen in my hand: "Mama, what makes you think *that*?"

"Oh, I don't know," she mused, putting down the dress. "Just a feeling."

"Well, feelings or not, I'm going out with him," I said, giving my hair one hard stroke. At the age of seventeen I felt I knew more about life than Mama did, and I wasn't going to let anybody tell me differently.

As a result, Sal and I went together off-and-on for a year and a half. Soon my dresser at home was covered with little gifts he had given me: a charm bracelet, earrings, a compact. One balmy summer evening after we had come home from a young people's get-together, we sat down on our porch swing. My brother David, who was chaperoning, felt we were on safe territory and went into the living room to catch a favorite radio program on the family Philco set.

And so Sal and I visited on our porch swing, a good three feet separating us. We got to talking about our futures, and for some reason I felt impelled to say, "Sal, as I may have told you earlier, my dream is to become a pastor's wife."

He started to speak, but he never had a chance to get the words out.

"What do you two mean sitting here all alone?"

Sal and I almost fell off the swing. It was Papa coming home from work. He stood at the bottom of the porch steps, hands on hips. "Do you realize all the neighbors are watching you?"

David came rushing out of the house, almost tripping over a house plant on the porch corner. "Pa, I'm here! I'm here!"

Papa snorted, shook his head and stamped into the house. But the spell was broken. Sal got up, tightened his tie and said, "Well, I've got to get ready for work tomorrow." He left.

If I worried that the confrontation with Papa had cooled Sal's ardor, I was wrong. He seemed more convinced than ever I would marry him. In the meantime we continued going to the young people's get-togethers at our church, where I played the violin. I didn't know a certain young man had been watching me until one day a friend and I walked home.

"Franny," said Dana, "someone's interested in you."

"What do you mean?" I asked, swinging my purse.

"Oh, a certain young man," she said, trying to be coy.

"You better tell me unless you want a purse on your head," I laughed.

"Well, it's a young man who originally came from a little town upstate. His name is Michael, and I hear he's been asking about you."

"Oh?"

"But you don't have to worry," she added quickly. "Somebody told him you were engaged."

"Engaged?" I stopped and drew myself up. "Where would they get *that* idea?"

"Well, everyone knows you and Sal have been going together."

"That doesn't mean a thing!" I huffed.

Three nights later at a Sunday get-together, Dana poked me in the ribs. "See, there's the boy I've been telling you about. He's looking at you."

At the far end of the room drinking punch was a

handsome young man who averted his eyes as soon as he saw me looking at him.

That evening, whenever I could, I stole glances at him. He was nice enough looking, but he seemed to have a certain self-assuredness about him. Almost a little cocky, I thought, the way he talked with some of the other young men, giving his opinions.

I mentioned this to Dana. "Maybe it's because he's in business for himself," she said.

"What kind of business?"

"Oh, I don't know...something to do with windshield wipers."

I sniffed. "Windshield wipers? Doesn't sound like much to me."

"Well, my brother says he's very ambitious, and he thinks he's going to be a real businessman someday."

"Well," I said, "you can forget him as far as I'm concerned. I'm going to be a pastor's wife."

In the meantime Sal talked more and more of marriage. It all came to a head one night while we were sitting on our front porch. My chaperone brother was sitting close to the door, focused on the radio; Fred Allen was giving one of his comedy routines.

"Fran," said Sal, "I got it all planned out. When we get married, we'll live with my mother and save money that way. Now, I know she's an invalid, but my sister and her husband will live with us too. Sis can take care of mother, and you can go to work."

Gripping the arm of the porch swing, I sat staring at the streetlight. All the years of working at home swirled around me—the scrubbing, the cleaning, the cooking. With Sal I would be jumping from the frying pan right into the fire. Mama, I realized, was perfectly right.

The next day I gathered up all of Sal's gifts and returned them to him. "I'm sorry, Sal," I said, "but, remember, I said I wanted to marry a pastor."

Only thing was, I still hadn't met a boy who planned to be a pastor. However, I was sure I would because our young people regularly went to rallies at other churches in Philadelphia. Somewhere I would meet the man God intended for me, I believed. And I continued praying that He would show me the one.

But the only one I found myself noticing at the rallies was Michael Cardone. I couldn't help liking his enthusiastic personality, the bright look in his eyes when he talked to someone. I noticed others seemed to feel the same way, including girls. And this, I had to admit, made me feel a little jealous.

One evening after I played the violin at a rally and it was drawing to a close, Michael came up alongside of me and asked, "Can I take you home?" I found myself answering yes.

"But we have to take my brother," I added.

"Sure," said Michael, as he carried my violin case to the car and the three of us headed for home. I had to admit I was thrilled he wanted to take me home. David fell asleep, which didn't seem to bother Michael at all. He seemed grateful for the chance to talk to me. When we arrived in front of our house, I did something I never expected to do.

"Would you like to come in for a cup of cocoa?"

David shot me a puzzled look. I had told him earlier I wasn't interested in this man. But Michael's brown eyes brightened. "Why, sure," he said. "It will be a pleasure."

My heart beat faster as we walked into the front door. Then I almost died. The living room was piled high with the dining-room furniture. Beyond it I could see the dining room jammed with our kitchen table, chairs and some cabinets.

"Let me see what's going on," I said in a weak voice, and picked my way around the furniture into the kitchen.

There was Papa in his undershirt on his hands and knees, laying linoleum. He looked up, his brow streaming sweat. "Hi, Francee, isn't it going to look beautiful?"

I smothered a sob and stumbled back into the living room. "I'm sorry our place looks so awful," I blurted. "My father's putting a new floor in the kitchen."

"Oh, that's fine," Michael said with a smile. "Your father must be quite skilled to do that."

His pleasant reaction to what some people would find an embarrassing situation put me at ease.

"Oh," I sighed with relief, "would you still like a cup of cocoa?"

"Sounds wonderful," he said. And with a heart strangely light I went back into the kitchen where Papa had just finished the job. I put milk on the stove and found myself humming happily. Papa was sitting on a chair drinking a glass of milk. Looking at me, he remarked, "Hmmm, something seems to be making you happy, Francee." He smiled and nodded toward the living room where Michael and David had set up chairs and were talking. "Could it be that young man out there?"

I shushed him. "No, Papa," I said, "he's just a friend." But I felt my cheeks reddening as I stirred the cocoa.

By the time I had learned enough to know that when you relinquish yourself to Jesus and let Him control your thoughts and actions through His Holy Spirit, you always seem to know just what to do and what to say at the right moment. I thought about this as I poured out the three cups of cocoa and put them on a tray with some cookies. This Michael Cardone knew just what to say and when to say it.

I carried out the tray to the two young men with the strange feeling that this would not be the last time I would be serving refreshments to the one I had called a "show-off businessman."

This Is My Story This Is My Song

Chapter Five

ROMANCE ON THE RIVER

I was in the kitchen helping Mama make macaroni with broccoli when my brother David rushed in. "Hey," he exclaimed, "what d'ya know? Your boyfriend just drove up in a *car!*"

I whirled and faced him angrily. "Boyfriend? *Whose* boyfriend?"

David backed off, his arms held out in surrender. "I...uh, I just thought..."

"Well, you had better think again," I snapped. "I don't have a boyfriend, and if you think that Michael Cardone is—"

"Hah! Got you!" he interrupted with a grin. "I didn't say *who* it was, and you automatically came up with his name. So...?"

My face flushed. I was struggling for an answer when the doorbell rang. I went to the door to find Michael Cardone standing there. Still ruffled from the confrontation with my brother, I could only manage a "Yes?"

Embarrassment crossed Michael's face for an instant, but he quickly regained his composure.

"Fran," he said, "there's a rally tonight at the church in Paulsboro. How would you like to go?" He pointed to a nice-looking sedan at the curb. "I would like to drive you there."

I was silent for a moment. Truth was I had already planned to go to Paulsboro since they had asked me to sing. But I didn't want to say yes too quickly.

"All right," I said finally. "But you'll also have to take my brother."

"Oh, sure," he smiled, his brown eyes lighting up. But before he could say anything more, my brother boomed out behind me, "Great! I've always wanted to ride in a car like that. That's a great-looking machine you have there, Mike." He rushed past me. "D'ya mind if I look at it?"

"Not at all," smiled Mike, who kept his eyes focused on me.

While David crawled all over the car, Mike and I made nervous conversation.

"Er, uh, looks like we might have some rain later," he said, looking at the sky.

"Oh, yes," I said, looking up too. "It does look like it." A long silence.

Then, "Uh, that's a nice-looking car you have."

"Yes," he said, "I just bought—"

"Hey! What you two standing at the door like that?" I turned. It was Mama, who had come out of the kitchen, tired, I'm sure, of our awkward repartee.

"Francee, don't you think you should invite the young man in?"

"Oh, sure," I flushed, opening the screen door. "Come in." I remembered Mama was at church the night Michael brought me home when Papa was installing the kitchen floor. I quickly introduced them to each other.

Mama was bustling back into the kitchen, clattering dishes. Michael and I sat across from each other stiffly. "Well," he said, "the Paulsboro rally is at eight o'clock. How would it be if I picked you up at seven o'clock? And David, too, of course."

"Fine," I began when Mama sailed into the room with a tray of cannoli and cups of cocoa. I was surprised; she had never demonstrated such hospitality when Sal came to the house.

After Michael left I mentioned this to Mama. "Well," she said, "I think he is the right one for you."

"Oh, Mama," I protested, "you know I'll never marry anyone but a pastor."

"Well," she said, shaking her head, "he has a kind face, and I feel sure he is a Christian."

Our trip to Paulsboro was not what I expected, with the three of us making a leisurely drive. When Michael pulled up in front of the house, I stared in shock. I had never seen so many people jammed into one car in my life. Kids were almost hanging out the windows. As David and I walked out to the car, I said, "Do you think there's room for us?"

"Oh, sure," said Michael. Realizing how the car looked, he added quietly, "Some of these kids have never met the Lord, Fran, and I thought it would be great to bring them to Paulsboro." He opened the door for me and whispered, "You can never tell what will happen."

The drive to Paulsboro was an experience in itself. I sat between Michael and a girl; I could hardly breathe. David was squeezed between two girls in the back, but he didn't seem too unhappy about it.

Everyone talked at once, excited about the rally. When Michael braked for a traffic signal, one of the young men in the back remarked, "Boy, Mike, your brakes are a lot different from those in your old Model A." I assumed he was talking about a car Michael owned previously. "Yes," said the girl next to me. "Every time he put on the brakes in that old car, it would shudder and dance before stopping."

"That's because the old Ford had mechanical brakes, Sally," said Michael, adding proudly, "this one has hydraulic brakes, and all four wheels work together under a pressurized system."

I had no idea what he was talking about. But I remembered he was in some kind of auto-parts rebuilding business. However, after we reached the Paulsboro church, I saw a side to Michael Cardone I never knew before.

At the rally I sang "In Times Like These" and noticed Michael watching me with a soft look in his eyes. An evangelist gave a rousing message about how the Holy Spirit can transform us if we allow Him to. "If we give ourselves completely to Jesus," he said, "we are filled with His Spirit, and through the Holy Spirit God can perform His work through us. He gives us abilities and power we would never have dreamed possible."

That night in Paulsboro I saw this happen through Michael Cardone. I watched him talk with some of the young people he had brought with us. A special light seemed to glow in Michael as he related what the Holy Spirit had done in his own life.

"You know," he told two young men, "I'll always remember a terrible experience I had when working for another company some years ago. I had thrown my all into the job and advanced to section manager. Then our superintendent told me I was in line for department supervisor. And I worked even harder."

"Did you get it?"

"No."

"Why?" asked one of the young men. Clearly they were fascinated.

"Because he gave the job to his wife's cousin."

"I'da punched him in the nose and walked out," said one.

"Well, I was tempted to do just that," laughed Michael, "but I had already put my trust in the Lord. So I forgave the guy; I knew what kind of pressure he must have had from his wife. Besides, I figured God had something better waiting for me."

"Did He?" asked the other youth.

"Sure," said Michael. "I figured this was my opportunity to go into business for myself. I already had some good training in remanufacturing auto parts and started up a little shop in my grandma's basement."

Michael looked over at me and continued. "My

brothers joined me in the business; we've been in operation over three years now, and we're doing all right."

"Wow," said one of his listeners. "I'd like to get that kind of confidence."

"You can," said Michael, "right now. All you have to do is accept the Lord Jesus Christ and *mean* it."

With Michael leading him, the boy repented of his sins and asked for God's forgiveness. Michael placed his hands on his head and prayed for him. Something seemed to happen to the kneeling young man; when he stood to his feet, a kind of glow filled him.

Suddenly I was looking at this Michael Cardone through new eyes. He seemed so much more than just one of the many young men I had come to know, much more even than a young, enterprising businessman. He was a man of God.

On our ride home I didn't talk much. My thoughts raced. *Just because he brought someone to the Lord, doesn't mean he is the one for me. After all, I had promised myself to marry a pastor.*

Michael pulled up in front of our house. Before David and I got out of the car, he asked: "There's a special evangelist speaking at Green Lane campground next week. Would you like to go?" Green Lane was an Assembly of God campground about an hour and a half from Philadelphia.

"Sounds wonderful," I replied, mentally berating myself for being so quick to say yes. But there was something about this young businessman I found attractive. And it wasn't just because he was such a worker for the Lord.

The next weekend we drove up to Green Lane along with, of course, a car full of young people. I figured I had better get used to the fact that when one goes out with Michael Cardone, one goes out with a crowd.

Green Lane was an exciting meeting, and the evangelist preached a fiery message. But something else impressed me. After he spoke, Michael turned to me. "Would you mind coming up with me while I talk with him?"

"Not at all," I said. Watching Michael Cardone relate to the evangelist was fascinating. I saw him give the evangelist some money as he said: "Remember, if you ever need a part for your car, just let me know." He added, "It'll be one you can depend on. Better than new."

On the drive home I glanced at Michael and found myself wondering. Does a man have to preach to be a minister? He certainly was doing the Lord's work, leading others to Christ and helping out pastors and evangelists whenever he had the opportunity.

I peeked at him as he steered the car down the highway. There was an air of assurance about this man, the kind you find only in someone who has put himself completely in the Lord's hands.

By the time the sedan pulled up to our house that night, I knew in my heart that Michael Cardone, in his own special way, *was* a minister. I also knew he needed a wife who would back him up in every way. And I knew that if he asked me to marry him, I would say yes.

Early one evening in July 1941, Mike (as I now called him) and I sat on a bench in Philadelphia's Fairmount Park overlooking the Schuykill River, where boathouses dotted the shores. A soft breeze blew up from the shimmering waters, betokening a special something in the air. Mike studied his hands for a moment, then turned to me.

"Fran, we've known each other for several months now, and I can't think of a better life than having you at my side. Will you marry me?"

My heart felt like it was bursting. I took his hand. "Oh, Mike, of course; I love you."

He kissed me, then smiled. "Even if I'm not a preacher?"

I laughed. "Mike, I think you are more of a pastor than many I know. I'll be proud to be your wife."

We didn't say anything for a moment, savoring the glow. Down on the Schuykill, two men got in a racing shell and with long easy strokes sent it gliding up the river.

As I watched them rowing together in perfect unison, I had a feeling that's how our marriage would be.

Then followed a very tense time. Mike invited me for Sunday dinner to meet his family. I was on pins and needles as he escorted me to the steps of his family's house in North Philadelphia, a nicer area than my neighborhood. We walked past the building which housed his auto-parts remanufacturing business to the residence behind it.

A sweet-faced woman met us at the door. "Mother, this is Frances," said Mike, and, turning to me: "This is my mother, Concetta." His mother gave me a big hug. Next I met Mike's father, Joseph, a merry-eyed man who called me "Honey." I was beginning to feel at home until Mike's mother led me to the table. I had already suspected what the main dish would be: manzani, long macaroni with holes in it, the traditional dish with which Italian mothers welcome their prospective daughters-in-law.

But I hadn't anticipated what it would be like to sit down at a table with Mike's four brothers and two sisters. All stared at me, none of them saying a word. It was like being in a goldfish bowl.

To overcome my jitters, I made small talk. It turned out that all of Mike's brothers were in his business with him, but conversation was still artificial. Mike's mother kept offering more manzani; I felt she suspected my slender physique wasn't substantial enough to make a good Italian mother. Mike's father tried to put me at ease, calling me "Honey" all the time. But I still felt ill at ease.

As it had done in the past, music saved my life. After dinner, we walked into the living room, where an upright piano stood against the wall. "Oh," I exclaimed, "who plays the piano?"

Heads shook silently.

I turned to Mrs. Cardone. "Do you mind if I play?"

"Oh, thank you! Thank you!" she cried. "It would be wonderful."

I sat down at the piano and began to play "Qual Grande Tesoro" (Marching to Zion). After a bit I began singing, and before I knew it all of the Cardones had gathered around, singing with me. I hadn't known it was Mrs. Cardone's favorite hymn. Now I really felt at home. We sang hymn after hymn.

Finally Mama Cardone called out, "Oh, we must

hurry. We have only a short time before we go to church."

Sunday evening services at the *Italiano Pentecostale* downtown started at 7:00 p.m., and it was a half-hour ride. With a flurry of activity, everyone got busy.

Mike came to me holding a tie. "I'm going to see how good at housekeeping you are," he laughed. "Can you press this?"

"I'll be glad to," I said. Taking it over to the ironing board, I placed the tie down, noted in which direction the fabric was woven and began ironing it on the bias.

He stared opened-mouthed. "Why do you do it that way?" he asked. "I just iron them straight down."

"This is how I was taught in fashion-design school," I said, explaining that it doesn't stretch the tie when ironed that way. I showed him the completed tie.

"Well, I'll be," he marveled, "it certainly looks better than the way I did it."

I didn't tell Mike I had won awards in fashion design. The Bible says something about boasting.

But there was no false modesty when Mike and I talked alone. We fell into an open, give-and-take conversation naturally. Perhaps in our case it was the Holy Spirit at work, but good conversation is something vital in any good marriage.

Our dates usually ended up at Friedman's Ice Cream Parlor on Snyder Avenue, where Mike and I enjoyed our favorite—strawberry ice-cream sodas. (David was so happy that his chaperoning days were over.) We talked about our favorite foods: macaroni with marinara sauce, calamari, escarole. As we passed these names back and forth, we were amazed to discover we both enjoyed the same dishes. How's that for the Holy Spirit bringing two people together?

However, aside from our mutual likes, I didn't know that I would also become a part of my fiance's business.

Some of our dates turned out to be "working" dates. One day when Mike drove up in his sedan, I noticed the backseat was filled with shipping cartons.

"Do you mind very much, Fran?" he asked. "I have to deliver these carburetors to a customer."

"Not at all," I said. I loved this man so much I would have helped him package those carburetors if he had asked me. Thirty minutes later we pulled up in front of Mike's customer, a distributor's warehouse.

Mike stopped the car and turned to me. "Fran, I'm going to have to carry this order into the warehouse in two lots." He cleared his throat. "Would you mind accompanying me with the first lot and watch it while I go back to the car for the rest?"

"Sure," I said. "But why?"

"Well, the last time I delivered here, I brought in thirty-six carburetors with the first lot. When I got back with the other half of the order, there were only eighteen carburetors sitting there. Of course, I couldn't blame anyone, but," he added, "I've got a good idea of what happened to them."

"I understand perfectly, Mike," I said, "and I'll be glad to be your watcher. After all, if we're going to be husband and wife, what's mine is yours and what's yours is mine. We're in this marriage together."

"You don't know how good that makes me feel!" he smiled. So when Mike carried in the first half of the order, I went with him and stood by it looking as determined as I could. The man receiving the order gave me a strange look, then busied himself with papers on his desk.

From then on, there were no more parts missing from Mike's deliveries. My first job with Mike as a "watcher" was a portent of interesting things to come.

Chapter Six

"LIKE APPLES OF GOLD"

By the time Mike met me at the altar of Calvary Temple (the former *Chiesa Italiano Pentecostale*) on September 28, 1941, he must have wondered if I was the same girl he had proposed to.

My weight had dropped to ninety-two pounds. I had been on a day-and-night schedule for weeks preparing for the wedding and making not only my going-away outfit, but also my mother's and sister's dresses. On top of that I had made all the drapes, spreads and curtains for the new house Mike and I had purchased in North Philadelphia. Now I almost rued the day I studied fashion design and dressmaking in school.

Even so, it was a thrill to make furnishings for that

house at 746 Garland. We were so proud of it. It cost all of $3,500. You could see all the way from the kitchen into the living room, and for this reason we called it the "Sunlight House." I think that was a fancy way of saying the house was small.

Thank goodness we had the reception in my mother's house. With all the people that came, I think our "Sunlight House" would have gone into eclipse. Happy guests partook of ham-and-cheese sandwiches, cookies and soft drinks. The only similarity between our modest reception and the extravaganzas young people have nowadays, was our presenting guests with the traditional Jordan almonds, which signify fertility.

We drove to Washington, D.C., for our honeymoon. Our trip was so short I think I spent more time packing and unpacking than seeing the sights. But Mike couldn't get away from his growing business any longer than a few days. Even so our little sojourn was peaceful and idyllic as we strolled past the big government buildings, the museums and monuments. We didn't have enough time to tour the Capitol or the White House. But I do remember stopping in front of the Lincoln Memorial one evening, looking up at the softly lighted statue of the great man seated there and thinking how he had said that during his deepest crises he had nowhere to go but on his knees. I thought how he started out in life as a poor farm boy, and through faith in God and hard work he had achieved the most eminent responsibility in the land. I looked at my new husband standing by me and thought how he, too, started out as a poor boy from a coal mining town and through godly faith and hard work was developing a successful business.

I squeezed Mike's hand, thinking how this kind of success story is what made our country so wonderful. There's no limit to what anyone can accomplish with faith in God, imagination and hard work. I was so glad my mother and father came here.

Before I knew it we began packing to go home. On our way home the fuel pump on our car gave out, but we were able to make it to a gas station. All the fuel pumps they had in stock were brand-new ones.

"No rebuilts?" asked Mike.

"Didn't know they were available," said the mechanic.

Mike reluctantly let him put on a new one, but not until he gave the station owner a sales talk on the value of a remanufactured fuel pump. As I watched him work, I could see why my new husband was such a good salesman.

"Now when you buy a remanufactured part from my company, you and your customer both benefit," he told the owner. "The car owner gets a part usually better than new at a lower price; you not only make a fair profit, but gain a happy customer who'll come back again."

The station owner nodded approvingly, and Mike gave him a list of his remanufactured parts.

"The way you were going at it," I said after Mike got back into the car, "I'm surprised you didn't also try to sell him on making a commitment to the Lord."

Mike put on the brakes. "You're right, Fran," he exclaimed. "I'm going back to do just *that*." Seeing the look on my face, he laughed and continued driving. "Just kidding," he grinned. "But, you know, Fran, you were closer to the truth than you think."

"When I make my sales calls, more often than not the dealer and I end up talking about the Lord. Practically everybody is hungry for Him, even though they may not know it."

Mike went on to explain, "I don't push it; I let the Holy Spirit guide me. Not long ago I called on a dealer near Scranton. As we talked I noticed photos of children on his desk and asked him about his family. I always want to let the customer know I'm interested in him personally, not just because of his business.

"Well, the poor guy shook his head and almost broke down. Turned out his seven-year-old boy just had an operation for a heart defect, and it didn't look like he'd live. I knelt down by that man's desk and prayed with him for his little boy right then and there.

"Afterwards, the dealer admitted he had never prayed like that before, adding that he normally left that kind of prayer up to his priest. 'But I got to say,' he said, 'hearing you pray for my little fellow sure helps me feel a lot better.'

"'God hears us when we pray,' I said, and assured him that I would keep on praying for his son."

Shortly after we returned home, Mike phoned the dealer and called me from work. "Fran, that little boy we prayed for is going to be all right!" he exclaimed. "Isn't that wonderful? Praise the Lord!"

I hung up the phone giving thanks not only for the little boy but for a wonderful husband like Mike. I truly felt like I was a pastor's wife.

Later, that new fuel pump we bought outside Washington, D.C., failed. Mike showed it to me before he tossed it into a pile of what we call "cores," old auto junk parts that come to his plant for remanufacturing.

"We'll take this broken-down pump and remanufacture it into a brand-new one, restored for service," he said. Then a light shone in his eyes. "Say, Fran, isn't this what Jesus Christ does with us? We come to Him broken down and worn out, and He restores us, makes us new again."

I kissed him.

Fortunately, I didn't have to work after we were married. Mike felt it was enough that I kept the home going. And by careful attention to our budget, I was able to make ends meet. I also knew that when children come home from school calling, "Mom! Mom!" there is nothing nicer for them to hear than a warm welcome. Of course, in those days it was easier for a wife to stay home. Today some wives have to work to make ends meet. In fact, I understand that over 60 percent of wives today have jobs outside their homes.

This can be difficult, especially when children are involved. My advice to a working mother is to take advantage of every moment possible to be with your children. Let them know you love them and want to be with them. To this end, except for church, a working mother should avoid all activities outside the family as much as possible. And even in church, a working mother should be careful to avoid things that take her away from the children. There'll always be enough time later. By all means involve the whole family together in good wholesome fun: picnics, trips to amusement parks, camping trips, taking them to church and Sunday school. Remember: by the time a child is nine years old, his or her life with you is half over. When someone first told me this, I bristled in disbelief. Then I realized it was true. When a child is eighteen, he or she is usually gone from the home already, into college or on his own.

However, as Mike will attest to, I was no stay-at-home wife. I was the organist at our church. No longer did we have services with everyone singing the old gospel songs in Italian. However, we still raised "sounds of joy," as the psalmist David wrote. And with services Sunday morning and evening, Tuesday and Thursday nights, plus choir practice, you can see where I spent a lot of my time.

Along with this I taught two Sunday school classes, including small children and young married women. This wasn't just limited to Sundays. Every month I would teach the young married women sewing, cooking and other skills, such as flower arranging and oil painting.

Sometimes Mike got home from work, dinner wouldn't be quite ready. And I don't blame him for complaining. There's nothing a man likes better than to find a hot, appetizing dinner waiting for him and a smiling, cheerful wife. I must confess that didn't always happen in our early years. After a long practice on the church organ or a session with the young marrieds of my Sunday school class, I thought I'd be so tired Mike would find a worn out wife just beginning to prepare dinner.

If it hadn't been for an old pastor-friend, Edward Menaldino, I don't know what would have happened. He gave me some advice I never forgot. "Franny," he said, "when you're married, always use the tone of voice that charmed your husband when you were courting."

So instead of barking back at Mike I remembered

Pastor Menaldino's advice. I think it saved ten thousand arguments. The tone of voice one uses with his or her spouse—or anyone for that matter—makes all the difference between a happy relationship and a sour one.

Married people get so used to each other that they often forget and let irritation, impatience or anger show in their voices. They don't mean to be hurtful, but it does rub the other person the wrong way; he or she responds in kind, and soon there is an escalation of angry words. The Bible says, "A word fitly spoken is like apples of gold in pictures of silver" (Prov. 25:11, KJV). This world is tough to live in. And no married couple can make it by disparaging one another. God says a husband and wife become *one,* and that's the only way they can make it. In union there is strength.

Courtesy is the oil that smooths relationships between a husband and wife. It reduces the friction in family relations. Courtesy even saves lives. A friend of mine knows Mario Andretti, the famous race-car champion. Mario says professional race-car drivers are very courteous to each other on the speedway. He says race-track spectators are not aware of the extraordinary number of "pleases," "thank yous" and "you're welcomes" passed between the drivers. And much of it is communicated through hand signals.

Drivers are courteous for one simple reason, he said: "It saves lives."

There's no race-track rule requiring it, but drivers warn each other of mechanical failures on other cars, indicate which side it is safer to pass on and signal lane changing. If a driver sees trouble on the road ahead, he raises a clenched fist to warn others behind him.

On public highways, the only hand signals Mario says he sees are obscene ones. But his heart lifts when he sees another driver being courteous, such as motioning another car to enter the line ahead of him. When this happens, he usually sees the second driver in turn being courteous to others. Courtesy is contagious. "There's an old Italian proverb, *Beretta in mano non fece mai danno,*" Mario says, which means, 'Cap in hand never did anyone harm.' Humility has a lot to do with courtesy—getting outside yourself, being considerate, making those small sacrifices, thinking of others first."

Yes, courtesy *is* contagious. I was standing in a long check-out line at the grocery store the other day. The overworked cashier was grumpy, and so were the other folks in front of me when she had to call the manager to correct a register error. When I reached her, I breathed a little prayer to calm my own impatience. I smiled and said, "A rough day, huh?"

The smile that shot across her face was worth waiting in line for. She exclaimed: "Oh, thank you for being so patient!" Before she finished ringing up my order, she was even humming a little tune. As I walked away I noticed she was welcoming customers behind me with a nice word and smile.

I was struck by the realization of the effect we have on others. So often we tell ourselves: "What I do or say won't make any difference." Yet everything we say or do ripples through the world around us for better or worse.

I'll never forget in fashion-design class one day, a fellow student who wasn't very popular was having trouble threading her sewing machine. Finally, one of the other girls stepped over to help her. Spurred by her action, two other girls joined in to help.

The effect of such little acts when multiplied by millions of people across our country every day are a tremendous power for good. For whatever I do, my brother or sister who sees me is so inclined to do. Psychologists call this "suggestion." In the Bible Jesus calls it "witnessing."

My point is, if we treat our spouse with the same deference and courtesy we give to a stranger we're trying to impress, our marriage can't help but be a happy one.

I'll never forget a powerful lesson I learned about witnessing shortly after our first child, Ruth, was born. As you can see, those Jordan almonds worked.

This Is My Story This Is My Song

Chapter Seven

A WORD FOR THE WISE

As it was, I wasn't sure our little daughter, Ruth, was going to make it. It began with a terrible accident at my sister-in-law's house. I was helping with her drapes. At six months' pregnant, and near the end of the day, I was getting weary. Finally it was time to go. I kissed my sister-in-law good-bye at the front door, turned and started down the concrete steps leading to the sidewalk. I should have held onto the railing. But it happened so quickly. My foot slipped, and I found myself falling. Terror filled me as I tumbled down the steps. I ended up flat on my back, staring at the gray sky, hearing my sister-in-law screaming in horror. All I could do was gasp: "Oh, Father, please protect my baby...please protect my baby."

My sister-in-law helped me up the stairs into the house, where I sat for a long time. The painful bruises and scrapes on my body didn't worry me. All I could do was pray that my child would be all right.

As I sat there I uttered a prayer that would be on my lips for the next several weeks. "Oh Jesus, cover my baby with Your precious blood." I believed I was praying one of the most powerful prayers a person could plead. My pastor had explained it to me.

When God spoke through Moses, He commanded His children not to eat meat with blood in it. That was because the essence of life was in the blood: "...for the blood is the life; and thou mayest not eat the life with the flesh" (Deut. 12:23). So even to this day, Jewish Kosher butchers drain the blood from the animal as they slaughter it.

God also tells us in Leviticus 17:11 (TLB), "For the life of the flesh is in the blood, and I have given you the blood to sprinkle upon the altar as an atonement for your souls; it is the blood that makes atonement, because it is life."

In Old Testament times Jewish priests sprinkled the animal's blood upon the altar as an atonement for the people's sins.

When Jesus died on the cross, the shedding of His blood was full and perfect atonement for all of our sins. And I believe there is no more powerful prayer than to ask our Lord to cover the person or need with His blood.

And so after that terrible fall, I prayed every day for the Lord to cover that little baby inside me with His blood. The baby thrived, but I wondered if the Lord had heard me when I gave birth prematurely a month later.

Little Ruth, born two months ahead of time, weighed only two pounds, twelve ounces; the doctor could hold her in the palm of his hand. But, leaning down with his stethoscope, he listened and lifted his head with a smile: "This little one has a strong heart; I think she will live!"

I breathed thanks and continued to pray for her every day. Even so, she lay still in her incubator and hardly seemed to grow. The doctor recommended that she be fed with an eye dropper, but it didn't appear to help.

One night, while standing by her with hot tears burning my cheeks, I felt someone at my side. I looked up to see the night nurse.

"You know, Mrs. Cardone," she said. "I had a premature baby like your little one, and I, too, tried to feed her with an eye dropper."

"How did she do?"

"Not well at all," she answered. "So I fed her with a bottle."

"And...?"

"She thrived on it." The nurse looked at me. "Can I try it with your baby?"

Somehow I had a feeling she knew more about "preemies" than anyone else connected with our case, and the Spirit within me responded "Yes!"

That night little Ruth started nursing from a bottle. Before long she was a fat, healthy baby.

As Ruth was a miracle baby, so was our son. Again, his life was saved because of advice from someone who was not an "expert." The night he was due, I agonized in the delivery room from intense waves of pain that made me scream. The baby should have appeared long before this, and though I was pushing as hard as I could, it was just not coming. "You're not trying, Mrs. Cardone!" the doctor barked at me. Shaking his head, he strode out into the waiting room and told my husband in disgust: "This woman isn't helping me!"

He returned to find an intern examining me. The young man looked up at him. "She is having a breech birth!"

Suddenly the delivery room came alive as the team of doctors worked to save our lives. Finally, using forceps, they were able to help our child into the world. Even so, the umbilical cord was wrapped seven times around its head, and the baby was blue. Again the doctors worked feverishly, and soon the newborn let out a healthy squall.

As I look back on that frantic time, I believe Satan did not want that child born. For he grew up to be a mighty Christian and an astute businessman who is now president of Cardone Industries. He was named for his father. I think in view of his battle it is fitting that he bears the name of Michael, the archangel who conquered the dragon, Satan (see Rev. 12:7).

As I think back on those days when two amateurs out-thought two experts, I always think of the scripture that says: "The foolish shall confound the wise" (see 1 Cor. 1:27).

With both Ruth and Michael to care for, our household was a busy place. And even in those hectic days I learned a lesson.

A young girl came over every so often to help me. Her father was Catholic and her mother Protestant, but neither went to church. As a result, the children had no interest in religion. The girl's teenaged brother, Roger, often accompanied his sister to help. It was through him I learned an important lesson in witnessing.

It happened on a day when I was both very tired and busy. I was rushing to the laundry, arms loaded with clothes and a box of soap. As I passed Roger, who was mopping the kitchen, he said, "Mrs. Cardone, I have to ask you something."

I halted impatiently. "What is it, Roger?" I asked over the clothes piled in my arms.

"How do you get religion?"

My shoulders sagged. Not only was this boy stopping me from my work, but he was asking questions many religious philosophers have been trying to answer for centuries. Moreover, I didn't think this teenager was serious. Just an idle comment, I thought.

I was about to shrug him off with an "I'm sorry, Roger, I'm too busy" when something stopped me. Today I'm sure it was the Holy Spirit. I stopped, took a breath and said: "Oh, we got saved"—and rushed on to the laundry.

A month later Roger came up to me while I was hanging clothes in the backyard.

"I have something to tell you, Mrs. Cardone," he said, beaming. "Now I *know!*"

"Know what?" I asked, taking a clothespin from my mouth.

"Remember the day I asked how you got religion?"
"Yes?"

"I wondered what you meant by 'saved,'" he said. "Saved from what? Drowning? A fire?"

He dug his toe in the grass, then looked up at me.

"Well, I took a girl out on a date shortly after that, and I brought it up in our conversation."

"So?" I was about to hang one of my husband's shirts on the line.

"Well, it turned out she was a Christian," he said with mounting excitement, and she explained *everything* to me, about accepting Jesus, confessing my sins and giving Him my life."

He took a deep breath. "And that's just what I did, Mrs. Cardone. I got saved, and now I know what you mean. I can't thank you enough for telling me!"

I stopped still, Michael's shirt flapping in the wind, feeling a mixture of emotions. Shame for not taking the time to sit down with Roger and really explain Jesus to him when he asked that important question. And a deep gratefulness to the girl who helped him. Most of all, I was in shock at the discovery of what my *one word* did in the life of another.

It was as if I was hearing the Lord's words: "So shall my word be that goeth forth out of my mouth: it shall not return unto me void, but it shall accomplish that which I please, and it shall prosper in the thing whereto I sent it" (Is. 55:11).

What did that one word *saved* accomplish? Roger grew up to become a very effective minister, leading thousands of people to Christ.

Yes, the power of God's Word is dynamic, no matter who speaks it, no matter the situation and even if it is taken lightly. Once spoken, it never returns void.

Jeremy Levin, one of the Americans held hostage in Lebanon, says he was an atheist when captured. To keep himself from going crazy, he thought about all his experiences in life. The things that affected him most were words, words of street-corner preachers he used to shrug off, words of television evangelists before he angrily turned off the set. They were words that got him reading a Bible and finding Jesus Christ in captivity. Today he continues to work for the Lord.

Yes, words can have a powerful effect. An example I find thrilling was told to me by a friend who knows a man in Ohio named Terry Sternad. Terry, who considered himself an atheist, had a five-year-old son, "T.J.," whom he loved deeply. Terry carpooled with a co-worker, Don, a Christian, who talked to Terry about how Jesus loved him. Terry kept shrugging him off.

Then tragedy struck. Little T.J. fell through the ice of a pond and drowned. At the hospital, while holding his son's body, Terry was hysterical with grief. In desperation he phoned the only person he felt could help him. Yes, it was Don who rushed to the hospital and prayed with the distraught father. Terry found a strength and comfort he had never known before. Today he and his wife minister to other couples who have lost children.

I feel so sorry for those who hear His words but do not accept them. In fact, I used to wonder about Matthew 20:16: "...for many be called, but few chosen." It sounded like God was being choosy.

How could some people make it to heaven and others not? One day a minister gave me an illustration that made it very clear to me. Over the doorway to heaven is a big sign announcing: "Everyone invited!" When those who decide to step through that door turn around, they see another sign above it on the inside:

"Congratulations, you have been chosen!"
I look forward to seeing that sign.

Chapter Eight

THE CARBURETOR

I sat by my father's bedside as he was dying and held his thin, worn hands—hands that had spent a lifetime serving others. My father had served his adopted country as an American doughboy in World War I, and through the years afterward he had served his fellowman as a waiter in such notable hotels as the Bellevue Stratford and Warwick. Proud of his profession, he had followed the biblical injunction: "Whatsoever thy hand findeth to do, do it with all thy might" (Eccles. 9:10). And Papa did just that, serving people in a way that pleased them and made them feel comfortable. Among his guests were such men as Herbert Hoover and Franklin D. Roosevelt. And yet, I know Papa served his lesser-known guests with the same courtesy and grace he bestowed on V.I.P.s.

When Papa died, I feel sure he was greeted by the Lord's words: "Well done, thou good and faithful servant" (Matt. 25:21).

Though I lost my father, the Lord continued to bless our family as Ruth and Michael grew physically and spiritually. Of course, we suffered the usual small crises that go hand-in-hand with child rearing. Michael Jr. got scarlet fever and was quarantined for twenty-one days. His father had to live elsewhere during that time. When Mike said, "I really missed your cooking" I didn't know whether to take it as an insult or a compliment!

The time came for us to move from the Garland Street house to a larger one. We were all looking forward to a place where we wouldn't be bumping into each other. But after the movers left I found myself walking around our little "Sunshine House" with a poignant feeling. So much had happened here—the beginnings of our family, get-togethers, dinners. I would always be grateful to it. I placed my hand against the wall and breathed a little prayer of thankfulness for it to the Lord and that He would bless the new family moving in.

Ruth and Michael both began taking piano lessons. Ruth, I believe, inherited her love of music from me. Not only was she singing as a small child, but she applied herself to the piano and also mastered the organ. She played so well that when we had company, we'd gather around the instruments and sing hymns.

Michael? What he inherited wasn't from me. He got as far as mastering Rachmaninoff on the piano. Then, feeling his task was completed, he never touched the keys again. But Michael had inherited something from his father that stands him in good stead today.

I saw it beginning on my kitchen table. I was washing dishes while musical notes from Ruth practicing at the piano drifted in from the living room. My husband and little Michael sat at the kitchen table with their heads together, talking quietly. I leaned over to see what they were doing and recoiled in horror. On my clean table sat a dirty, black metal thing. My husband picked it up and was about to point out something to his son when I exclaimed, "What is that terrible thing doing in my kitchen?"

"Oh, don't worry, Fran," said Mike. "It's an old carburetor from a Briggs & Stratton lawnmower engine. I'm showing Michael how to make it like new."

"Yeah, Mom," said my son, "Dad's going to show me how to *remanufacture* it!"

"Not on my clean table, you won't," I warned.

"Oh, Fran," pleaded my husband. "Look, we spread newspapers over it and," he patted Michael Jr. on the shoulder, "if our son is going to take over the business someday, it's time he started learning how."

I glanced at Michael Jr. The excited look in his brown eyes melted my heart, even though he already had a grease smudge on his cheek.

"Well, all right," I said, "but please be careful."

As the two worked together, I couldn't help peeking over their shoulders occasionally. Under my husband's guidance, little Michael was carefully taking the carburetor apart with pliers and a screwdriver, laying out pieces of it on the newspaper. I left the kitchen to see how Ruth was doing at the piano. As I watched her following the score, a pungent odor—coming from the kitchen—struck me. I rushed in, demanding, "What is making that terrible odor?"

My husband looked up. "Oh, cleaning solvent, Fran. We have to wash the grease and dirt from each part to see which have to be replaced."

I threw up my hands, closed the kitchen door and retreated to the living room, wishing little Michael had maintained his interest in the piano. "At least it didn't smell so bad," I muttered to myself.

"What?" asked Ruth, her hands lifted from the keys.

"Oh, nothing," I grimaced, "but don't go into the kitchen for a while unless you want your sinuses irritated."

Sometime later, Michael Jr. marched into the living room proudly bearing the carburetor, which he had reassembled. Its bronze casing glowed almost as brightly as the look in his eyes. "Look, Mom," he said, "it's *better* than new."

My beaming husband stood behind him. I couldn't decide who was prouder of what: little Michael of the carburetor, or big Michael of his son.

Later, after the children were in bed and we had aired out the kitchen, Mike talked enthusiastically: "You should have seen the little guy, Fran. He worked so carefully with that carburetor, disassembling it, cleaning the parts, replacing worn fittings with new ones."

Mike stopped for a moment and stared into the distance, as if seeing the future. "I kind of feel like King David when he knew his son Solomon was going to finish the temple he had dreamed of building."

Mike took my arm and faced me. "Now I know our

son is going to take over our company someday and make it even better than I could envision."

I kissed him. "I like your dream, Mike, but please clean that grease off your forehead before you come to bed."

He placed that little bronze carburetor reverently on a shelf in our living room. And every time I dusted it, I had a feeling it held a special significance in our family's life.

About this time Mike's father died. For years Joseph Cardone, also a deeply committed Christian, had suffered a wracking cough from "black lung disease" due to his many years of laboring in the coal mines of eastern Pennsylvania. Finally it took him at age fifty-six. As he lay dying, he called for me. "Francee, come here." Taking my hand, he said, "Make sure everybody takes care of Mike." Somehow he felt a special concern for Mike, perhaps because he was the oldest of his sons. Mike shook his head sadly. "When we said good-bye to Dad as he left for the mine in the morning, we didn't know if we'd see him alive that night. And so we'd always place him in God's hands."

Mike brushed a tear from his eye. "And now...as he leaves us on a much longer trip, I take great comfort knowing He *is* in God's hands."

Mike was proud to be the son of a coal miner.

Perhaps that is why Mike and I were so close to our children. We had loved our parents so much that it spilled over to the next generation. Some people say you should never be that close. I say "phooey" to that.

For this reason, when Mike and I planned a long-dreamed-of trip to Europe, we decided to take little Ruth and Michael with us. Well-meaning friends couldn't understand this. "Why burden yourselves with the children?" they asked. "All they'll want to eat is hamburgers, and soon they'll start asking when they can go home."

But we were adamant. Somehow it was important that the children accompany us. Off we went. We rented a car and drove through France, Germany and into Italy. Realizing how bored they could get by just sitting in the backseat of the car, we took pains to acquaint them with the upcoming areas we'd be traveling through. For example, by the time we got to the Eiffel tower, they already knew about Gustave Eiffel, the genius engineer who designed the intricate supportive framework that holds our Statue of Liberty together.

As we visited castles along the Rhine, explored the catacombs of Rome and glided along the canals of Venice, I felt we became even closer as a family. Sure, the children were cranky at times and were more captivated by the pigeons in Venice's St. Mark's Square than its fabulous cathedral, but all of us carried home warm memories that will far outlast any costly souvenirs other parents bring to stay-at-home children.

Even today, Michael Jr.'s eyes light up as we talk over old times. He'll exclaim: "Say, Mom and Dad, remember that time you held me on your shoulders so I could see?"

The highlight of our trip was meeting with Uncle Giovanni, who had returned from America back to Troia, his and my parents' hometown, as a missionary serving the people there.

We had taken a car ferry from Genoa down to

Naples, where Uncle Giovanni would meet us at the dock. The only problem was I had not seen him since I was a child and had no idea what he looked like. How would we recognize him? It was solved by the one trademark he always carried with him. I'll never forget that Sunday afternoon as our ship edged into the pier at Naples, the Mediterranean sparkling behind us. There, among the crowd of welcomers on the dock waving and shouting greetings, we easily picked out Uncle Giovanni. How could we tell? He was waving his large Bible, which he always carried with him.

As I thought of the wonderful work this fine Christian man was doing, I remembered another man I had learned about while visiting the Coliseum in Rome, that famous amphitheater where so many Christians were martyred.

After our guide took us to the foot of a large cross which now surmounted the Coliseum, he told about the terrible orgies of cruelty and killing that went on to "entertain" the people in the days of the Caesars. In the midst of one such horrible event, an elderly Christian saint stood up and shouted out to the Roman emperor ensconced in his royal box how wrong this barbarism was in the sight of God. The outraged emperor ordered that the old man be brought down to the Coliseum floor, where he was executed.

As the story goes, a solemn hush hung over the amphitheater. Instead of cheering raucously, the spectators one by one filed out of the stadium, to the bafflement of the emperor. And, according to our guide, never again were the cruel orgies and gladiator combat held in the Coliseum, all because of one man standing up for God.

It's amazing what one man can do. But a man can also fall from grace if he allows himself to succumb to Satan. I learned this when our family was viewing Leonardo da Vinci's famous painting "The Last Supper," which adorns a wall at *Santa Maria delle Grazie* in Milan. The guide said the artist chose a local young man who had the face of a saint to model for the portrayal of Christ. He found others to model for the apostles but looked long and hard for a depraved-looking person to model for Judas. As he began to paint him, he made a starling discovery. This was the very same person who had modeled as Christ years before. However, since then he had lived a sin-filled life. The effects of it showed on his face.

It reminded me of an old saying I heard often from my mother: At age sixteen we have the face God gave us; at age sixty we have the face we have given ourselves.

Everything depends on the choices we make in life. Mike and I have always felt a deep responsibility in helping our children make the right ones. Of course, we know the ultimate decision for Christ must be made by each individual. As the old saying goes, you can lead a horse to water but you can't make him drink.

Even so, we endeavored to do all the leading we could. We made sure our children were in Sunday school every week and summers found them in church camp. Those were blessed times when, after arriving home from camp, Ruth and Michael (each at different times, of course) ran up to me, calling: "Mom, I got saved!" As I saw that special light in their eyes, I thanked the Lord. I knew there still would be pitfalls and hard lessons ahead for each. But I also knew that in making their commitment, the die was cast. They belonged to Jesus, and He would see them through.

In leading children to the Lord, I always remember the example of a renowned violin teacher in England. He believed in going to the hospital when a child was born to play his instrument to that baby until the child was old enough to take lessons.

"They have to get it in their ears," he explained. It's the same with Christianity. You must get it into their ears—let them hear the music, the preaching, as babies. As they grow, it will become as much a part of them as the roots are of a tree.

Along with this, however, expect a certain amount of rebellion from your child. It is only natural for them to want to assert themselves. And often they will strike out at the thing you cherish most: your own faith in Jesus. But don't fight back with them; give them all your love and continue to pray for them. Remember, you have planted the seed of Christ in them. And, come what may, it will grow and flourish.

One spring I was intrigued by what was happening in a certain spot on our blacktop driveway. A stray seed had germinated below the surface of the macadam topping. The next week it had broken through the hard blacktop, pushing aside little chunks of pavement in its quest for the sun.

I firmly believe that is what happens when you plant the seed of Christ within a child. It will germinate and flourish and, eventually break through the hard exterior of the world in its quest for the Son.

This Is My Story This Is My Song

Chapter Nine

REACHING A DECISION

W e were having dinner one evening when my husband said something that caught my heart. "Well," he said as I poured him another cup of coffee, "seems like our Ruthie has an admirer at work."

Admirer? I knew our daughter was going steady with a young man, but he didn't work at Cardo, my husband's business, where Ruthie was now employed. Truth was, I had just become accustomed to Ruth's dating, and now to learn that *other* young men were interested in her?

Oh, Ruthie, I thought, *my little girl.* I looked at Mike. He had a twinkle in his eyes; I wanted to tell him to put a stop to anyone approaching our daughter. But, of course, I realized she was no longer "little Ruthie." She had grown to be a lovely young woman. After high school she had attended Bible college but then decided she wanted to support herself. I think she inherited her work ethic from her father. So she came home, and since Cardo needed a secretary, she applied and got the job.

I enjoyed Ruth being home. More than a daughter, she had become a close friend. We spent many hours together talking about the Lord, our family and her brother, Michael Jr., who seemed to be feeling his oats. Ruth always patted my hand and said not to worry, it was just a phase Michael was going through. "Remember," she said, "he gave himself to the Lord, and *that's* permanent."

But most of all we talked about our common love, music. Not only did Ruth play the piano and organ at home, but she would often be found at the organ at Calvary Temple.

"He brings her coffee quite a bit." My husband's words broke my reverie, and I sat up. "*Who* brings her coffee?"

"Oh, a young man who works in the factory," he said, sipping his coffee. "Seems a nice enough fellow."

"What's his name?"

"Ruben. Ruben Tarno."

"Well," I said, "he probably doesn't know Ruth is going with someone right now."

"Maybe he does and maybe he doesn't," said Mike, "but one thing is sure, he's a persistent young man."

When I next visited Mike's factory, I made it a point to notice Ruth's admirer. He was a tall, good-looking man with curly hair. When he stopped by Ruth's desk, I could see her eyes light up. I knew right then that the other young man didn't have a chance.

And Ruben *was* persistent. Before we knew it Ruth was proudly showing us her new engagement ring.

They had a beautiful wedding at Baptist Temple. While there I overheard a comment which emphasized the fact that looks are deceiving. Ruth was of a diminutive stature, standing only four feet, eleven inches tall. At the reception, as I was standing at the buffet, I overheard a tall, stocky woman sniff, "She'll *never* have children."

A year after the wedding, Eric was born. Roger came three years later, followed by Patricia twelve years after that.

Meanwhile, as the Lord giveth, He taketh away. My brother, David, who was so stalwart a chaperone for Mike and me in our early dating days, died at a relatively young age. He had never fully recovered from an illness he contracted in Europe during World War II.

His death left us grief-stricken, and I had a difficult time understanding why such a think would happen.

I was also deeply concerned over our son, Michael Jr. He would soon be going to college. I couldn't help but hope that he would choose a Christian college. This was during the sixties when most secular colleges had become infiltrated with "Flower Children" and recreational drugs.

"Michael, have you thought about a Christian college?" I asked one day at the table.

He looked up at me as if I had asked him to work on a rubber plantation in Malaya.

"Oh, Mom," he grimaced. "You know I'm a Christian, but I don't want to go to one of those places where guys wear string ties and the girls go around in gingham dresses and high-top shoes."

"But, Michael…" I started to press, and then noticed he was looking at a folder from one of the major universities, which was lying next to his plate. Michael was exceptionally skilled in gymnastics. In fact, Syracuse University had already invited him there because of this.

What can I do? I wondered to myself. I even went so far as to slip a little Bible under his mattress. "Jesus," I prayed, "I give my son to You. Please lead him to a Christian college."

A few days later I walked into Michael's room to find him standing there with a quizzical expression on his face and holding up the little Bible. "Did you lose this, Mom?" he asked. He had a twinkle in his eye, the same one I saw in his father's when he kidded me.

I was at my wit's end. "Lord," I pleaded, "I've asked You to help Michael be receptive to a Christian college, and it seems he's going just the opposite way. Where are You when I need Your help?"

It was then I felt Him speaking to me: *Don't you trust Me, my child? I have heard you prayer. But be patient; allow Me to work.*

It brought me to my senses. I had gone to God and given Him my plea. When He didn't work as fast as I wished, I stamped my foot like a small child. I was learning that when I put something in God's hands, I must let Him handle it in His own wise way, and not grumble or be impatient if I don't get an answer to my prayer right away. His time, I learned, is not our time.

Sometime later I heard a speaker tell a story which underscored this lesson. Seems there was a man who had a once-in-a-lifetime chance to talk directly with God.

"Lord," he asked, "is it true that to You a million years is just a minute?"

"Yes," said the Lord.

"And is it true that to You a million dollars is just a penny?"

"Yes, My son."

The man rubbed his hand together greedily and said: "Then give me a penny."

"In a minute," answered the Lord.

The story was a lesson that spoke to impatient people like me. And so I relaxed and let God work. But I did keep on praying. Even Michael seemed to notice my new attitude. "What's the matter, Mom?" he said one evening at supper. "How come you—" He shut up and continued eating, afraid, I'm sure, of breaking the spell.

Meanwhile, the Lord worked in His mysterious way.

One day I walked into our family room to find Michael watching Merv Griffin on television. The famous TV host was interviewing Oral Roberts, who was just starting his new university in Tulsa, Oklahoma.

My son watched, transfixed.

Something prompted me to say, "Michael, why don't you think about going to that new university?" Then I caught myself, remembering I had promised not to push my son, but only pray.

He didn't say anything, but he didn't explode either.

He just kept watching the two men talk.

A short time later my husband had to make a business trip to Tulsa.

"Say, Michael," he said, "how about coming with me. We can see some of the sights on the way. And they tell me Tulsa is an interesting city."

"Sure, Pop," said Michael. I remained silent and prayed.

In a few months Michael Jr. was registered in the first class to go through Oral Roberts University.

Again, I learned a lesson. When you push things too hard instead of depending on the Lord, there's a danger of pushing them right out the door.

As much as I celebrated Michael Jr.'s going to a Christian university, there was a mixed blessing. He insisted he could not find any spaghetti sauce as good as mine in that "Wild West city." As a result, I soon found myself in the Cardone mail-order business, preparing quarts of my spaghetti sauce and mailing it to Tulsa.

How could he eat so much of it? I wondered, as I packed up what seemed to be the umpteenth container of sauce to take to the post office. I found out when I went out there to visit. One of the reasons my son was so popular on campus was because he took my sauce to his friends' houses, where they cooked up huge pots of pasta.

"Mrs. Cardone," said one young student, "you ought to market that wonderful sauce commercially. I know it would go over big all across the country." I didn't tell him I did not want to be another Mama Leone. I had enough to do at home.

For whether I wanted to or not, I was becoming

Frances and Michael Cardone pioneered an Automotive Parts Remanufacturing Company, now the world's largest privately-held Remanufacturer.

Michael and Frances, 1943.

Baby Frances with her parents
Ponziono and Jennie Lizzi.

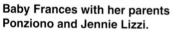

Frances and Michael
Cardone on their engage-
ment June 1, 1941.

**Frances and Michael on their Wedding Day,
September 18, 1941.**

Frances and Michael at their 50th Anniversary Party.

Our son, Michael Jr., now President
& C.E.O. of Cardone Industries

The Michael Cardone, Jr. family; left
to right, Ryan, Michael, Jr., Michael III,
Jacquie, and Christin.

Grandson, Michael
Cardone III

Granddaughter,
Christin Cardone

Grandson, Ryan
Cardone

Granddaughter,
Patricia Tarno

Ruth, "My Daughter, My Friend," went to be with the Lord on January 10, 1990.

Grandson Eric and Lisa Kay Tarno with great-grandson, David Brandon.

Michael and Frances' daughter, Ruth, shown with her husband Ruben, sons Roger and Eric, and daughter Patricia.

Grandson Roger Tarno, his wife Miriam, great-granddaughter Julie Danielle, and great-grand-son Jeffrey Roger.

Our 50th Celebration

500 guests assemble in the Grand Ball Room of Hotel Atop the Bellevue to honor Frances and Michael at their 50th Anniversary Party.

THANK YOU
by Ray Bolz

I dreamed I went to Heaven and you were there with me;
We walked upon the streets of gold, beside the crystal sea;
We heard the angels singing - then someone called your name,
You turned and saw this young man and he was smiling as he came.

He said, "Friend you may not know me now," then he said "But wait!
You used to teach my Sunday School when I was only eight;
And every week you would say a prayer before the class would start;
And one day when you said that prayer, I asked Jesus in my heart."

"Thank you for giving to the Lord,
I am a life that was changed;
Thank you for giving to the Lord,
I am so glad you gave!"

One by one they came, far as the eye could see;
Each life somehow touched by your generosity.
Little things that you had done; Sacrifices made;
Unnoticed on the earth - in Heaven now proclaimed.

Our six grandchildren presented us with a special song "*Thank You*" at our 50th Anniversary Party

Eric

Christin & Ryan

Michael III

Patricia

Roger

Michael Cardone, Sr. has built the largest privately-held automotive parts remanufacturing business in America on the principles of God's Word.

On February 8, 1970, Michael Cardone, Sr.'s birthday, M. Cardone Industries was born at 3911 N. 5th Street, Philadelphia, PA.

Aerial view of the 20 plants with over one million square feet that make up the operating facilities and general headquarters of Cardone Industries, Philadelphia, PA.

Christian Life Center dedicated in memory of our daughter, Ruth, in Bensalem, PA.

Christian Life Center Sanctuary, Interior View

The Vice Presidents of Cardone Industries presented my husband with this eagle during the Automotive Hall of Fame Ceremonies.

Frances pictured with her family and Dr. Paul Yonggi Cho during a special meeting at Cardone Industries.

Frances and Michael pictured with the late Dr. T. F. Zimmerman and Dr. G. Raymond Carlson, former General Superintendents of the Assemblies of God.

Michael and Frances greet Dr. Billy Graham at the Fort Lauderdale Crusade, 1987.

The Assemblies of God presented my husband with a bronze cast sculpture of Jesus washing the feet of his disciple. (pictured with us is Dr. Del Tarr, President of the Assemblies of God Seminary)

At the Automotive Hall of Fame Reception, my husband and I were presented with an artist's rendering of the Michael & Frances Cardone Building, the new home of the Assemblies of God Theological Seminary, in Springfield, Missouri.

Michael and Frances Cardone, Sr. with their children and grandchildren.

Frances and Michael pictured with Dr. and Mrs. D. James Kennedy, of the Coral Ridge Presbyterian Church, Ft. Lauderdale, Florida.

My Husband was inducted into the Automotive Hall of Fame in September 1994, joining other industry leaders including Henry Ford, Walter Chrysler, Carl Benz and Lee Iacocca.

Henry Ford

Lee A. Iacocca

Michael Cardone, Sr.
Industry Pioneer and
Founder of Cardone Industries, Inc.

Walter Chrysler

Harvey S. Firestone, Jr.

Carl Benz

Here he is shown making his acceptance speech at the Westin Hotel, in Detroit, MI.

Thomas A. Edison

Frances joins other family members for groundbreaking ceremonies for a new plant.

At a Cardone employee event, Frances is presented with roses.

Dr. and Mrs. Norman Vincent Peale and Mr. and Mrs. Michael Cardone, Sr.

Frances has been a faithful church organist for over 40 years

The Frances Cardone Conference Room at the Michael Cardone Media Center, Springfield, MO.

The Frances Cardone Hall at Oral Roberts University was named in her honor.

This plaque is displayed at Oral Roberts University in the buildings which were named in honor of Michael and Frances Cardone.

Oil Paintings by Frances Displayed at Calvary Temple, Philadelphia, PA.

"The Harvest is Great but the Laborers are few"

"Calvary Temple"

"The Good Shepherd"

more and more involved in my husband's business. At dinner one night I could see he was particularly distressed. He picked at his food, and his thoughts seemed far off; he was very quiet. I had a good idea of what was bothering him. He was having an increasing number of disagreements with his brothers, who were partners with him in Cardo. I suppose if I had been one of those wives who put their husband on a pedestal and bowed to him instead of God, I would have avoided saying anything that might disturb him. Trouble with those wives is that when a husband, being human, lets them down, they fall apart. But if a wife puts her trust in God, she is given the strength to help her husband when he is in trouble. After breathing a prayer for guidance, I said: "Mike, when you don't touch my macaroni, I know something's wrong."

He sighed. "Oh, Fran, I didn't want to bother you with it."

"Mike," I said, "the Lord put us together for a reason, for me to help you and you to help me. We're a team; I'll stand with you all the way."

He smiled at me. "You don't know how good that makes me feel, Fran. But this is something I have to decide for myself."

"Well, let's talk about it," I pressed. "We're not making any decisions tonight."

Mike looked at me, his eyes twinkling. "You know, Fran, you missed your calling. You should have been a psychiatrist."

"Well, from what I hear about them," I laughed, "I think I could be just as good."

The humor seemed to lift Mike's spirits, and he

opened up. "My big concern is our son, Fran." He began eating his macaroni, talking between bites. "You know the company rules that no family member can become a part of the business. Well, that leaves Michael out. And ever since he was born, it has always been my dream that the two of us work together."

He took a sip of water. "Oh, sure, I know Michael has the brains and gumption to make it in any kind of work elsewhere. He's already listed in the *Who's Who of Colleges of America*. But I can think of nothing better than the two of us working together."

I nodded, remembering the two of them, heads together working on that little carburetor on this same kitchen table.

Talking seemed to do my husband a lot of good that November night in 1969, and he was in a better mood as we prepared for bed.

However, in the middle of the night something awakened me. I reached over to Mike's side of the bed to find him gone. My heart caught. It was a cold fall night, and through the bedroom window I could see dark tree branches swaying in the wind. Where was my husband?

I got out of bed and went to the head of the stairs. Then I heard him. He was downstairs, pacing the living room floor. I knew he was thinking about the business and his son. Not wanting to disturb him, I crept back to bed. About an hour later he returned, took off his robe and got into bed. Soon he was sleeping peacefully as if he had reached a decision and his mind was at rest.

The next morning as I hung up his robe, I felt something heavy in the pocket. I reached in and pulled out the little bronze carburetor he and Michael had worked on years before. As I held it in my hand, I knew Mike would soon be telling me his decision.

This Is My Story This Is My Song

Chapter Ten

FAITH ON FIFTH STREET

S o it was that November evening in 1969 that my husband came to me to discuss his decision.

"I was up doing a lot of thinking last night," he started.

"I know," I smiled. "I found that little carburetor in the pocket of your robe this morning."

And that's when he asked me what I would think about his leaving Cardo to start something new.

"I want your honest thoughts, Fran," he pleaded. "Will you be willing to go along with me? To help, to work with me? I couldn't do it without you being with me all the way."

He rose from his chair and started pacing the floor.

"It's going to cost us my salary, our medical coverage, life insurance, just about everything."

I looked up from the dress fabric I was sewing. His face was tense with anxiety. We'd be giving up security, an assured income and, most of all, comfortable retirement years in which we had long looked forward to doing just what we wanted.

"Are you sure, Fran?" he pressed.

I laughed. "Mike, I came naked into the world, and naked I'm going out. Of course, I'm with you." That pledge has not wavered since.

As I look back on that night, I realize now only God could have given me such faith and courage. And that was because He knew the future.

Though Mike's contract with Cardo wouldn't be up until his fifty-fifth birthday, February 8, 1970, it was as if a tremendous load was lifted from his shoulders. He no longer had that haunted look. Now his eyes were full of optimism as he planned what his new business would be.

Of course, I knew it would have something to do with rebuilding automobile parts. His talent for this had been obvious ever since he began rebuilding vacuum windshield wiper motors in a repair garage at age eighteen.

Mike had never done anything else—except work for the Lord in our church and teach Sunday school. His priorities in life were the Lord, his family and his business, in that order. I was proud to stand by his side when he was honored "Churchman of the Year" by our denomination, the Assemblies of God.

Now, as he began planning a new venture, I saw a

freshness in his face I hadn't seen in years. His dream was to start his own company.

"Right from scratch, Fran," he said excitedly one night at dinner. We'll all work in it together. And when Michael graduates from college, he'll come in with us."

I had never seen him happier. However, I wasn't sure what "We'll all work in it *together*" meant.

"You mean I'll work in the company too?" I asked.

"Sure, Fran," he said.

"But what can I do? I'm just a housewife. All I know is art and music."

"Fran," said Mike, putting down his fork. "You've got more common sense and brains than many so-called executives I know." He glanced around the room. "Look, you run this family, this house, like clockwork." He hesitated for a moment, his eyes glistening.

"I've got to tell you something, Fran," he continued. "Ever since you said you'd be with me all the way the other night, I couldn't help but think of what the Scripture says about wives like you." He opened the little Bible he carried and read. "Here, Proverbs 31: *'A good wife who can find? She is far more precious than jewels. The heart of her husband trusts in her, and he will have no lack of gain. She does him good, and not harm, all the days of her life'"* (RSV).

He put down the Bible and looked at me. "That's you, Fran. And if you think I can start up a company without you beside me, you have another thing coming.

"That's the trouble with Cardo," he continued. "No wives were allowed to have a say in that business."

I had to smile; he was so right.

"So," he said, placing his hands flat on the table,

"right off, you're my partner." He sat back and looked into the distance. "But partner in what? We don't have enough money to launch a new company, or even a building. In fact," he said ruefully, "I don't even know what kind of auto parts we'll remanufacture."

I knew Mike wouldn't go into products that Cardo or other firms were already rebuilding. His challenge would be something new. The answer to that challenge came soon.

On a rainy evening as I was preparing to put dinner on the table, he burst into the house carrying something the size of a softball wrapped in newspaper.

"I think I found it, Fran!" he called. Shedding his raincoat and hurrying into the kitchen, he laid the package down on my kitchen table with a metallic clump. Opening up the newspaper, he proudly displayed one of the ugliest things I have ever seen—old, black and greasy.

"Mike," I exclaimed, "get that awful thing off my clean table!"

"Fran," he beamed, "you're looking at the start of our new company!"

"It looks more like the *end* of something to me," I observed dryly.

"That's just it," he said, rewrapping the thing and putting it on the counter. "I'll tell you about it at dinner."

As we ate, Mike related how his windshield wiper motor had stopped working that day. He drove into a service station expecting to buy a rebuilt one only to find there was no such thing. He had to settle on a new one, but brought the old part home.

"After dinner I'm going to see what I can do with

it," he said. He was so excited he passed up my baked apple for dessert. And while I cleaned up the dishes, he spread newspapers over the kitchen table. After placing the old wiper motor on it, he sat down and started working.

As he bent over it, wielding pliers and screwdrivers, I couldn't help remembering another scene some fifteen years earlier when he and our son, heads together, worked on that little carburetor.

Finally, when I was putting the last dish back into the cupboard, he pushed his chair back and looked up at me. "Fran," he beamed, "I think I can do it." I leaned down and kissed him. "Mike, for thirty years I have believed you can do anything!"

"Thirty years," he sighed, "a long time. Say," he said, taking my arm, "do you think an old guy like me can start over?"

I laughed. "Old? Remember when we were in Florence and were so impressed by that beautiful Medici Chapel? Michelangelo started that when he was your age, fifty-five. And remember the Sistine Chapel? He was in his sixties when he painted that famous Last Judgment scene there."

"See," laughed Mike, grabbing my hand, "I told you I needed you."

Today, as I write these words, I have to agree with a statement by Ken Dychtwald, who counsels businesses serving the aging. He says middle age is "the most powerful and glorious segment of a person's life."

I think it's unfortunate that some people retire to doing nothing. Sure, some jobs are difficult, and the individual deserves a break. But the happiest people I know are the ones who go on to something else. I just read a study by Lydia Bronte, a researcher at Phelps Stokes Institute in New York, who completed a five-year study of one hundred fifty people ages sixty-five to one hundred two. She says: "Many people are as active as they've ever been during those years," pointing out that a lot of them changed their careers in their middle years. "The single most important thing," she observed, "was that they found work that they loved."

My husband, I was sure, had found the work he loved. But now it was up to me to find a place in which to begin our new venture. Mike was still tied to his desk at Cardo until February. Since Jesus warned us in Luke 14:28 always to count the cost before starting a project, we carefully assessed our finances and felt we could afford $4,000 for a building.

The first real estate man I went to became excited when I told him we were looking for a small place in which to start our business.

"Now here are some real possibilities," he said, flipping through his multiple-listing book. My heart sank as I noted the prices; we might as well have tried buying the General Motors plant in Detroit. When I told him what we could afford, his smile vanished and he shook his head. "I don't think you're going to find *anything* at that price in the Philadelphia area," he said. His phone rang; he picked it up and began talking. I waited a bit until it became obvious he had no more interest in me. I got up and quietly walked out.

Other real estate agents were just as hopeless.

"Mike, we've got a problem," I told my husband that night, relating my visits to the agents. "Maybe we should think about using our basement. After all, you started Cardo in your grandmother's basement."

"No," said Mike, "I believe there is just the right building waiting for us. If God put this idea into my heart, then He has a place for us. We've got to pray that He'll guide us to it."

Right then and there we placed our need in the Lord's hands, believing that He would lead us to the right place at a price we could afford.

But in the days following, as I drove up and down Philadelphia streets praying to be guided, I began to wonder if He didn't have in mind for us a barn down in Kentucky. *That,* I felt, we could afford.

One afternoon I found myself down Fifth Street. *Oops, not here,* I told myself, braking the car to turn around. It was a rundown neighborhood, and I couldn't imagine finding *anything* here. But for some reason I continued driving down Fifth Street past grimy storefronts, many of them boarded up. The buildings looked old enough to have been Benjamin Franklin's print shop.

Some blue and white colors caught my eye. Nearing them, I saw it was a real estate sign: "For Sale." When I saw the old storefront building it was nailed to, desolate and empty, the windows opaque with grime, I shuddered and was about to drive on. But something stopped me. I remembered a verse from the Bible advising us not to judge by appearances. (See James 2:1-4).

Was I letting the outward appearance of this place affect me? I pulled an old envelope from the glove compartment and scribbled down the phone number.

As soon as I got home I phoned Mike at his office. "Call the Realtor," he said.

When I did, the real estate man didn't know what I was talking about. But as I carefully described the location, he said, "Oh, it must be that electrician's shop. Let me check my files." He left the phone for a moment.

"Yes," he said, after returning, "That old place has been on the market for quite a while."

"How much is it?" I asked.

"Well, I think he might consider an offer of $4,000."

My heart stopped.

"Can we look at it this afternoon?"

"Sure," he said.

Later that day, Mike, the Realtor and I stood at the door of 3511 N. Fifth Street. It took the man some time to wrestle open the door. "Been a while," he said, smiling over his shoulder. Finally he creaked the door open. A musty odor assailed my nostrils. I glanced at Mike, but he had that hopeful look as we stepped inside. The Realtor pressed a switch. In the weak yellow illumination from the one dust-covered light bulb, all I could see was one horrendous, dirt-covered mess. Old scrap wiring, motor parts and other junk electrical equipment filled the shadows. Cobwebs festooned everything. Ancient wood boards creaked under our feet as Mike and I tentatively followed the Realtor, who made his way to the rear. "This place has a basement too," he announced cheerfully. Rusted hinges squalled as he pulled upon the door.

"Watch your head," he warned as he started down, holding a flashlight. I followed Mike, praying that the sagging steps wouldn't collapse under us.

At the bottom of the steps, the smell of earth, old wood and other indefinable odors was almost overpowering. Lights down here need to be connected," said the Realtor, playing the flashlight beam around crumbling brick walls and earthen floor.

I screamed. Two yellow eyes glared at us from a corner. I grabbed Mike, and the eyes disappeared with a scuttling noise.

"Just a rat," observed the Realtor matter-of-factly. Mike squeezed my hand. "Don't worry, Fran," he said. "Once we get this place fixed up, you won't recognize it."

"Sure, Mike," I answered, trying to keep my voice from trembling. The strange thing about it was, I knew in my heart this was the place God had picked out for us.

This Is My Story This Is My Song

Chapter Eleven

A FAMILY AFFAIR

I dipped my sponge into the pail of warm water with ammonia and started washing the front window of our new factory" at 3511 N. Fifth Street. It was late fall of 1969, and the first home of A-1 Remanufacturing[1] was humming with activity.

We scrubbed floors, and Mike was getting lights working in the basement, where much of our remanufacturing would be done. We had already spent days cleaning out the junk and scouring walls, floors and ceilings. Our new quarters were beginning to look respectable.

With one last swipe, I cleaned the remaining dirt from the window and stopped for a moment, admiring the view through it. The afternoon sun flooded Fifth

Street, and I thought it didn't look nearly as bad to me as when I first drove down it some weeks ago.

Then I saw him—a man in ragged clothes standing some doors away swigging from a bottle in a paper sack. He tossed the bottle away and staggered around the corner. I breathed a prayer that somehow Jesus would reach him, and remembered a little story one of our pastors had told us.

Two speakers in a public square—one communist, the other Christian—were arguing their own points of view before a small crowd of people. The communist pointed to a derelict garbed in filthy clothes slumped against a lamppost and shouted, "Communism can put a new suit on that man!"

The Christian waited for a moment, then responded: "Jesus can put a new man in that suit."

I looked around our shining new quarters and realized that was just what we had done here; the basic walls, ceilings and floors were the same, but Jesus— whom we had invited into 3511 N. Fifth—had given it an entirely new personality. He had become our Partner.

Before we had started our little production line in the basement, all of us gathered in a circle and dedicated every part of the business to God in the name of Jesus Christ. He was the One in charge, and everything we did would be under His guidance. That included every present and future employee, each part we produced and, of course, tithing.

Yes, though Mike and I had always tithed our income, we felt if God was in charge of this business, part of its profits would go to the Lord's work. When Jesus told us, "Give, and it will be given to you: good measure, pressed down, shaken together, and running over" (Luke 6:38, NKJV) we didn't think God's good measure would necessarily be in money, but rather in guidance, in wisdom, in the pleasure of His presence and also His healing and strength. This seems to work, for I had read where William Colgate, the soap manufacturer, gave ten cents of the first dollar he ever made to the Lord and became so successful he started giving half his income. Heinz of pickle fame, Baldwin, who made locomotives and Kraft, the cheese man, were also tithers.

Of course, they prospered because they also gave of themselves in producing not only the finest products possible, but in offering their customers exemplary service. And that was Mike's goal. "I want A-1 to be known for service, quality and availability," he said.

"I understand service and quality," I said, "but what do you mean by 'availability'?"

"There's nothing an auto-repair shop owner hates worse than finding out the particular part he has ordered is out of stock," he answered. "Not only does it mean a disgruntled customer, but it knocks his whole repair schedule out of kilter."

From the start we stressed "availability." I'll never forget the very first order. Mike was still at Cardo, but Michael was home from school on a holiday, happily at work on our little assembly line in the basement. He and Ruben had cleaned and disassembled the wipers, installed new parts and set them up in gleaming rows. I answered the phone, opened the mail and made coffee. Often, when our daughter, Ruth, was able to get a baby-sitter, she'd come into the factory and help me. I loved her presence. Through the years Ruth had become more than a daughter. She had become my best friend. If I was worrying about something, she would know just what to say to make me feel better.

When our first order came for three units, I thanked God for it. Then I carefully packed and rushed them to the post office. As I stood in line at the window, holding the package, I silently prayed not only for the wiper motors to reach their destination safely and to fulfill their function, but also for the well-being of the customer.

This was an extra ingredient customers got with their Cardone-remanufactured product. And though none of them knew about the prayer, they must have appreciated the service, for soon we were getting a lot of repeat business.

In fact, orders arrived to the point where we had to hire a few more people. Now we had a real payroll to meet. Not just family members were working at A-1, but people from the outside who depended on us for a living.

Worry seeped into me. At night I'd awaken in the wee hours and lie there fearful of what might happen to our fledgling company and the people who worked for us. Psychologists say our minds are most susceptible to worry in the dark hours of the night, when every negative thing looms larger than life. I personally believe Satan takes this opportunity to work on us. But thank God I knew what to do. When fears and worries attacked me like dark spirits, I called on the Lord Jesus. I would picture Him standing over me with outstretched hands, and hear Him say: "Cast your burdens upon Me."

And I would do just that, give Him all my worries and fears. Invariably, I would relax and fall asleep. Jesus never fails.

At the same time I found I could take a burden from my husband. Though he was still fulfilling his presidency at Cardo until February 5, he was handling all the books for A-1. However, the only time he could do this was on weekends.

One Saturday afternoon I walked into our study to find him surrounded by a sea of bills, statements and invoices. He looked so tired. I stepped behind him and placed a hand on his forehead.

"Mike, you work all week. To have this on top of you is too much. Show me what I can do."

He turned and looked up at me quizzically.

"Yes," I said, "I know I can do it." *With God's help,* I added silently.

He sighed and took my hand. "What a woman you are. Ok, go upstairs and get some shoeboxes," he said.

Wondering what he had in mind, I collected all the empty ones I could find and carried them down. Then he asked for a knife.

A knife? I wondered as I went to the kitchen for it.

Mike took the knife and cut a wide slit in the side of each shoebox. Then with a heavy pen he marked one "Invoices," another "Statements," a third "Bills" and so on. That's how I started doing the bookkeeping for A-1.

Later, it was time to give our records to our controller, Mr. Mattarazzo. His secretaries stared at me when I walked into his office. I could just hear them thinking: "Who is this crazy woman with all those shoeboxes?" After Mr. Mattarazzo finished his work, I returned, and he escorted me out into his office in front of his staff and complimented me. "You did a fine job, Mrs. Cardone," he said. "I knew where everything was."

Talk about "A word fitly spoken is like apples of gold in pictures of silver" (Prov. 25:11)! I was on cloud nine for days afterward.

But I do have to say how thankful I was when Jacquie came to help me. Yes, Jacquie, our new daughter-in-law.

Years earlier I had wondered if Michael Jr. would ever get married. Oh, he was a popular young man in high school, but he was no Don Juan. After he went to college, I suppose I should have realized something serious was going on when he sent us a photograph of a group of beauty-contest winners at Oral Roberts University. On the back was this cryptic notation: "The girl in the second row on the right, Jacquie Martin. I'm taking her out."

How nice, I thought, reminding myself to write Michael that she looked like a sweet girl. When I showed the photo to Ruth, she nodded knowingly. "Mom, I think you might be looking at your future daughter-in-law."

"Oh, Ruth," I said, brushing the thought aside. "You know Michael; he isn't *that* serious about girls yet."

She smiled. "Don't say I didn't tell you."

I sat down holding the photo and thought. It seemed only yesterday Michael was pedaling his tricycle around the backyard, bringing home attendance pins from Sunday school and getting into little-boy trouble. Why, it seemed only yesterday he had entered high school.

And now…a girl? Suddenly I felt very old.

Father, I breathed, *You know how much my husband and I have prayed that our children would be led to the right mates. If this lovely girl is Your choice for Michael, we thank You. If she isn't, please block the relationship.*

The Lord gave me His answer a few months later when my husband and I traveled to Oral Roberts University for a parents' weekend visit. All the way there I kept wondering: *What will she be like?*

I remembered how before Michael left home for college I jokingly told him, "Look, Michael, if you find yourself getting serious about someone out there in Oklahoma, make sure she's a nice Christian farm girl." He had laughed.

Not long after we arrived we attended a parents' reception. The mother of one of Michael's friends whom I had come to know asked me: "Would you like to meet Jacquie Martin?"

"Oh, yes," I said, "where is she?"

She pointed to a girl across the room, and my heart almost sank. This girl looked so sophisticated and was even more attractive than her picture. Would she be at home in an old-fashioned Italian family like ours?

"Well?" My friend broke into my thoughts.

"Oh, yes, I would like to meet her," I replied, a bit flustered. We walked across the room, and my friend introduced us. One look into Jacquie's eyes and my doubts vanished. I could see the spirit of the Lord in her. Realizing she must be ill at ease meeting her boyfriend's mother, I immediately tried to make her feel comfortable.

"My, it's easy to see my son likes beautiful women," I said.

She blushed and responded so warmly that I found myself feeling at ease. Soon we were chatting like old friends. I laughingly told her of my telling Michael to find a nice Christian farm girl.

"Well," she chuckled, "in a way I am." It turned out her father, a county judge in Fayetteville, Arkansas, also ran a poultry processing plant.

"Ask me anything you want about chickens," she laughed.

In 1969 Michael and Jacquie were married at Calvary Temple in Philadelphia. I was so grateful our son had found such a wonderful girl. Sometimes mothers can be very selfish and can't understand how wonderful it is that their sons are so happy. Jacquie is like a daughter to me, and in our twenty five years together we've never had a misunderstanding. One of the reasons for this, I'm sure, is because we have always respected her and Michael's privacy.

Of course, our whole family was at the wedding, including Mike's brothers, who had been his partners at Cardo. Naturally, there was some coolness between them when Mike announced he was leaving Cardo. But despite their business disagreements, I had no thought of *not* inviting them to the wedding. His brothers and sisters were family, and, despite everything, they always would be family.

One of the greatest tragedies in families is when members won't speak to each other. Of course, there will always be misunderstandings and arguments. But the sanctity of the family must be preserved nonetheless. What is more precious than love and forgiveness between brothers? Isn't this what Jesus asks of us?

A poem I came across recently says it very well:

Ah, friends, dear friends,
as years go on and heads get gray,
how fast the guests do go!
Touch hands, touch hands,
with those that stay.

Strong hands to weak,
old hands to young,
around the Christmas board,
touch hands.

The false forget, the foe forgive,
for every guest will go
and every fire burn low
and cabin empty stand.

Forget, forgive,
for who may say
that Christmas day may ever come
to host or guest again.
Touch hands! Touch hands!
(William H. H. Murray)

As the years progressed, all of us Cardones were very grateful that we had touched hands.

---

[1] Later to be incorporated as Cardone Industries, Inc.

This Is My Story This Is My Song

Chapter Twelve

GROWING PAINS

A tremendous roar shook our building, and a dark shadow crossed my desk. I turned to the window to see a huge semi-truck trailer pulling up outside. *Oh,* I thought, *he's making a delivery to some local business.* The front door opened, and a big, husky man walked in, papers in his hand.

"Who's in charge here?" he called out.

"I am," I answered, thinking he needed help in finding an address. "Can I help you?"

He stepped over and put the papers on my desk. "I got a delivery of twenty thousand wiper-motor cores for you, lady," he said. "It's C.O.D. I need a check for $9,052."

I stared at him. *Twenty thousand wiper cores? Nine*

thousand fifty-two dollars? "There must be some mistake," I choked.

"No, lady," he said. "I got it right here." He stabbed a beefy finger at the invoice. It bore my husband's name.

"Excuse me," I gasped. I got up and went to the basement door and called for Ruben, who was working on our assembly line. He rushed up the stairs.

"Do you know anything about twenty thousand wiper cores Mike ordered?" I asked.

He shook his head.

There was only one thing to do. I went to my desk, picked up the phone and dialed Mike, who was still working at Cardo.

"I...uh...oh...yes," he stammered. "That's right, Fran. I ordered those cores from Chrysler."

For a moment I couldn't say anything.

"Fran...Fran?" he pressed. "I'm sorry. I should have told you. I made a good deal with Chrysler Corporation to buy their surplus wiper cores they got back under warranty."

"Yes, you *should* have told us, Mike," I sighed, shaking my head. "Now tell me: What are we supposed to do with them?" I glanced around our little premises and shuddered.

He directed us to pile them up around the edges of our rooms. "Otherwise those old floors will collapse under the weight," he said.

I hung up the phone and told the driver where to put them. As his helper and Ruben began lugging them in, the driver said, "All I need is your signature on the invoice, Mrs. Cardone, and a check for $9,052."

The check! We had only $9,500 in our checking account. I dialed Mike again. He seemed unperturbed. I was shocked at his equanimity over what I considered a disaster.

"Go ahead," he said. "Write it out."

"But...you know it will clean us out."

"That's ok, Fran," he said. "Write it out."

With a shaking hand I did as he directed and handed the check to the driver, who wished us well and left. The building tremored again as the truck pulled away. Our little place was silent as Ruben and I stared at cartons stacked up against the walls. Then we looked at each other, and we both saw the same thought in each other's eyes. It looked as if Michael Cardone Sr. had made a big mistake this time.

I remembered my statement about leaving this world naked and wondered if it wasn't happening more quickly than I had thought. When Mike's brothers and other business associates heard about the twenty thousand wiper cores, they all shook their heads. One said that Mike was crazy.

Crazy like a fox, we learned later.

Mike worked out a loan, and along with some incoming funds from a few orders, we managed to eke along, as Job said, "by the skin of our teeth" (see 19:20).

But those orders were so few and far between it looked as if our little company would go broke before we really got started. Mike, on his own time, wore the tires off his car looking for customers. Each time he'd return home more and more dejected. I told Ruth how concerned I was for him.

"Don't worry, Mom," she said, patting my arm.

"Daddy doesn't give up easily." But I worried about him anyway.

One terrible rainy night as he took off his dripping hat and coat I could tell he was in a bleak mood. I had been keeping his dinner warm, and as he slumped down at the table his mind seemed to be in another world. Finally, I broke the ice.

"How did it go today, Honey?"

No answer.

Silence.

It would have been easy to get up and walk away from the table, saying, "All right, if *that's* the way you want it"—and clam up for the rest of the evening. But I had always remembered what a pastor friend told me before Mike and I got married.

"Frances," he asked, "do you believe marriage is a 50/50 proposition?"

"Of course," I answered, knowing I would always go halfway.

He shook his head. "You're wrong."

"What is it, then?" I asked.

"It's a 100/100 proposition," he said. "There can be no halfways in marriage. The husband and wife must each be willing to go *all the way* on their mate's behalf and not wait for the other to meet them halfway."

I had not forgotten that lesson. And so at the dinner table that night I gently prodded Mike. "Honey, I know you've had a bad day, and I'm here to help you."

Mike put down his fork and looked at me, tears brightening his eyes.

"Fran, I guess I'm just ashamed to admit it. But I think we've put all our eggs in the wrong basket.

Nobody seems to want remanufactured windshield wipers."

He looked so low I got up and put my arms around his slumped shoulders. "Mike, didn't we pray for this venture?"

He nodded.

"Well, what is there to worry about then? If God directed us into this, He must have a way of getting us through it. Remember what Jesus told us: 'I will not leave you comfortless: I will come to you' (John 14:18)."

Mike took my hand and looked up at me. "Fran, when the Scripture writer wrote that a good wife is far more precious than jewels, he was thinking of you."

That night we did a lot of praying about our problem. And, as always seems to happen after prayer, we came up with some ideas. One was allowing the dealers to stock remanufactured wiper motors without risk and let them see what happened when they offered customers a better-than-new wiper motor at less cost. In addition, we also decided to run some advertisements in automotive trade journals. And this is where my art training came in handy. I did some of the layouts and illustrations for those first ads. Not only did our new dealers' incentive plan and trade-journal ads start bringing in business, but I enjoyed seeing my handiwork published. In fact, later when we had a booth for A-1 Products at an automotive trade show, I not only helped design the booth but created oil paintings of our remanufactured parts. I was certainly no Rembrandt, but, then, what did Rembrandt know about windshield-wiper motors and brake cylinders?

In thinking back on that time when Mike's spirits sank so low, I am reminded of how a wife must be there to hold up her husband's arms when he's in trouble. She must be as Aaron and Hur were to Moses at that famous battle when the Israelites fought the powerful army of Amalek (Ex. 17:10-13). As long as Moses stood atop the hill with the rod of God in his hand, Israel was winning. But as he tired and his arms sagged, the enemy began winning. So Aaron and Hur stood on each side of Moses and held up his hands until the Israelites crushed the enemy.

I found myself holding up a lot of other things at our little plant as well. One cold, stormy Friday evening I was locking up when a truck pulled up outside and a man came to the door with a paper for me to sign.

"Cores," he said. "You folks ordered them."

Uh-oh, I thought, *Mike's been at it again.* But, of course, I knew cores were the lifeblood of our business. Signing the delivery slip, I said: "You can stack them in the storeroom." I pointed to the rear.

He shook his head. "Lady, they're out on the curb. We got to go." With that, he jumped into his truck and roared away. I stood in the doorway open-mouthed, staring at a small mountain of dirty, greasy cores stacked on the curb. An icy wind splattered sleet down Fifth Street. I knew those cores couldn't stay out overnight; they'd be gone before morning. What to do? I prayed. There was no one I could call at this particular time; Mike was on a business trip.

As I stood there I heard a noise behind me and turned to see Jesse Dawkins, our core man.

"Don' worry 'bout them cores, Mizz Cardone," he

said. "I'll take care of 'em." He stepped out to the curb, picked up some cores and carried them back to the storeroom. Sleet flecked his curly black hair as he came in with the cores. There was only one thing to do: I put on a pair of work gloves and went out there too. Back and forth we went to that greasy, ice-cold pile of metal, lugging cores into our storeroom. Finally, after two hours, with my apron and gloves black and greasy, the cores were all safely inside.

Of course, the staff found out about it. Not only did my experience breed a new sense of camaraderie, but it made me feel more a part of the business. It was also an education in recognizing the varying characteristics of different cores.

This came in handy in the case of the counterfeit cores.

In the auto-parts rebuilding business, a customer normally brings back old, used cores for which he gets cash credit from the company which originally supplied them as remanufactured parts. Such a shipment had come into us, and I was about to issue the usual credit when something stopped me. Call it women's intuition or the Lord's nudging. Whatever, something urged me to take a closer look at those cores. At first glance they looked like ours, with the familiar greenish paint. But as I examined them more closely, I discovered they were not our original cores at all. The people expecting credit had repainted them to look like ours. Of course, they didn't get credit; what they got was a directive to pick up their phony cores, pronto.

I felt pretty proud of myself until Mike started calling me "Sherlock." "I'll tell you something, Mr.

Executive," I replied. "I'm getting a little tired of being the only one in charge around here. I can't wait until *you're* here when some impatient trucker unloads a mountain of cores in the street."

Mike patted me on the back. "I know, Fran, I know what you've been through holding down the fort while I'm finishing up at Cardo. But, look," he pointed to the calendar, "in only two more weeks I'll be on hand full-time." That would be February 8, 1970, Mike's fifty-fifth birthday.

When that day came, my sigh of relief could be heard, I'm sure, all over Philadelphia. I felt a lot more secure with my husband next to me. And I found nothing more enjoyable than working side by side with him. In those days I was a Jack—or should I say, Jill—of all trades, working on the assembly line, in the office and doing both packing and shipping. Of course, I wore an apron to protect my clothes, and this caused me some hurt feelings. It happened when I overheard some women whispering about me. "Look at that Frances Cardone," one said. "Her husband is a company president, and she has to go around wearing an apron."

What hurt wasn't the fact that I wore an apron but that someone would consider it degrading. To me an apron signifies honest, hard work, something of which anyone should be proud.

When Mike found out how I was feeling, he put his arm around me and said: "Don't worry about them, Fran. Just let them watch you laugh all the way to the bank."

I was about to answer, "What bank?" for profits were still mighty lean in those early days. But I knew that when Mike talked about "going to the bank," he was something of a prophet. I was confident in his far-seeing wisdom. Take the case of those twenty thousand wiper-motor cores from Chrysler when many said he was crazy. He was thinking ahead to the time when such cores would not only be less plentiful but more expensive. When we were thinking in amounts of "twos and threes," he was thinking in terms of thousands. For, as it turned out, that giant delivery of wiper-motor cores was one of the best investments Cardone Industries ever made.

Other people also saw this certain "something" in my husband. I'll never forget the day one of our pioneer sales representatives, Walt Sullivan, brought a prospective customer into our little Fifth Street row-house "plant." The prospect was Lou Nulman of Alden Auto Parts Warehouse, who could mean a sizeable amount of business if he liked us.

I walked out of my office to greet them. After Lou Nulman glanced around our tiny offices, I could see him casting a quizzical look at Walter Sullivan as if to say: "Just *what* have you gotten me into?" And when Walter had to use a flashlight to lead Lou down the creaking steps into the basement to meet Mike on the assembly line, I thought that would be the last we'd see of Mr. Nulman.

Instead, I was surprised to find that he asked Walt to write up a sizeable order. Later, Walt told us: "Lou was so charmed by you folks. And he admired Mr. Cardone for his courage to start a new business at his age."

"You know," he added, "Lou saw something in Mr. Cardone that told him he was going to be successful. He saw in your husband a vision that was not to be denied."

That vision Lou Nulman saw was based on guidance from God. And it was on this foundation that Cardone Industries was based, rather than Wharton School of Commerce principles. This vision pertained to recruiting workers too. Mike always endeavored to sense how an employee's talents could best be used. For he knew this would not only make the person more valuable but happy in his work. And happiness is what we wanted first and foremost for our employees.

How this can work out can be seen in one of our first women employees. Lydia Kasakov and her husband had come from Brazil. He worked for us, and they lived in an apartment above our row-house plant. As yet they had no children, and Lydia did not know English. As a result she hibernated in their flat. I felt led to go upstairs and try talking with her. With my Italian and her Portuguese, I found I could reach her a little.

"Why don't you come down and work with us?" I offered. "You would not only find it interesting but a way to pass the time. And you could make some extra money to buy a dress and other things you want."

She was shy, but finally she came down and worked with me. Lydia caught on quickly, and soon she began to pick up English. It wasn't long before she was learning the catalog numbers of our products. And that was no small list, for by now our expanding company had branched out into power-steering pumps and distributors, each including a wide variety of models.

I was later to find out what my help meant to her in a very dramatic way.

Another addition to our staff came in May 1970

when our son, Michael Jr., came on board after graduating from Oral Roberts University. His sweet wife, Jacquie, who had been teaching school in Tulsa until Michael graduated, also joined us and began helping me with the books.

What a thrill to see my husband and his son now working together, fulfilling Mike's dream. One morning as I watched them, heads together, discussing the best way to set up a new assembly line, my mind raced back twenty years. Again I was seeing the two of them at our kitchen table, rebuilding that little carburetor.

In fact, they had never really separated since that time. When Mike sent our son to General Motors carburetor training school at the age of fourteen, I couldn't believe it. "Mike," I had questioned, "he'll be working with grown men there. How will he get along?"

"Don't worry, Fran," said my husband. "I think he knows as much about auto parts now as I do. He'll get along fine."

Michael did get along fine, and now he was proving invaluable at Cardone Industries. He was perceptive too. One morning he came to me: "Mom, with the way we're growing, we're going to need more space."

"I know, I know," I said, glancing around at our crowded premises. "Your father and I have talked about it, but things have been so busy we just haven't had the time to do something about it."

"OK," he said, "but we can't wait too long."

I meant to bring this up again to Mike, but after some urging I had finally been able to persuade him to take a long-delayed vacation.

It was an icy November up north when we left for

Florida. Mike and I had a wonderful week together. Of course, he took advantage of the quiet to work up some new catalog pages, but since he did it beside the pool, I didn't object. He was also getting some sun, and the lines in his face were beginning to soften.

On this particular morning the weather was especially beautiful. We had just come in from a stroll on the beach watching the sun break through the clouds over the Atlantic. As we stepped into our motel room the phone was ringing.

As the Bible says, trouble can come like a thief in the night.

Chapter Thirteen

OUT OF THE ASHES

I perched on the edge of the motel bed, heart pounding, as my husband talked on the phone. "Was anyone hurt?" he asked. Then his shoulders sagged with relief, and he whispered at me, "Everyone's OK." Turning back to the phone, he said, "Don't worry, Michael, don't worry. Let it burn."

As he tried to console our distraught son, I sank onto the bed overwhelmed by the immensity of our loss. *Everything* we had strived for, *everything* Mike had put us on the line for, was gone. Suddenly the loss was too much for me; I broke into sobs, rocking back and forth.

Mike glanced at me, bade a quick good-bye to our son, came over to the bed and sat down next to me, his arm around my shoulders. "Fran," he soothed, "don't take it so hard. It's only a building."

I blinked through my tears, hardly believing my ears. Mike was completely calm about the catastrophe that had struck us. He gently rubbed my back. "We can start over," he said. "It's not as bad as that."

I look at this man who should have been consumed with anguish. Instead, he acted as if nothing had happened, as if our son had called to say one of our machines needed replacing. I realized with blinding clarity where my husband's treasure was: not here on earth where it could be destroyed by moth, rust or fire, but in heaven where his heart was.

He was not a slave to the world and its calamities; he had cast his lot with Jesus—which put him above all that. And I saw the real truth of that old saying about feeling on top of the world.

If Mike could feel that way, so could I. I dried my eyes and started packing. For my husband was already on the phone making airline reservations back to Philadelphia. We had much work to do.

On the plane returning home, Mike took my hand. "Feeling better, Hon?" I nodded, forcing a smile. "You know, Fran," he continued, "when we knelt by the bed and claimed that promise of Romans 8:28,[1] I had a feeling that something good is going to come out of this."

Good? I wondered. I turned my head to the window. Sure, I believed that promise, but it was difficult to see what good could come out of losing one's livelihood in a fire.

As we walked out of Philadelphia's International Airport, an icy wind cut me to the bone, and I thought of how uncertain life is. A few hours ago Mike and I were laughing as we strolled together in the warm sunlight of a Fort Lauderdale beach. Now with heads down we trudged against a bitter northern blast.

As our son drove us to Fifth Street the next morning, he told us he had already been working with fire inspectors and insurance adjustors. My heart went out to him; he had been on the job less than a year, and here he found himself in the midst of a nightmare.

However, as I watched him talk to his father about what he had been doing, I saw a new maturity in him. The old saying is true: *When the going gets tough, the tough get going.*

As we turned down Fifth Street I held my breath as we neared 3511. There was nothing left of the little plant which had become so much a part of me in the past year. Now fire-blackened timbers leaned crazily against charred walls laden with ice from fire hoses. I looked for my desk, which had become a second home to me. Finally I saw it—a shapeless, charred mound. Whatever had rested on it was now ashes. An icy wind whirled them into a small gray cloud which settled on my shoes. Suddenly I was overwhelmed with hopelessness. What was the point in going on? *Everything* was lost: our records, our equipment and our stock! All that was left were charred boxes.

Our phone had rung off the hook the night we got home from Florida. Caller after caller expressed sympathy. Some of the calls were from Mike's old partners, his brothers at Cardo.

"Mike, c'mon back with us," offered his brother Tony. "We need you. Forget what's lost. C'mon back with us."

When Mike told me about the call, I wondered for a moment. It made sense. Cardo was still operating; it needed him.

But now it was Mike's turn to hold up my arms. He read my thoughts and asked: "Fran, has God let us down yet? Has He forgotten us through the years?"

A vision of our charred plant swam before me momentarily, but then it was quickly replaced by a picture of our good marriage, our son and our daughter with their families. Of course God had been good to us. If He had seen us safely through the last thirty years, He would certainly see us through all there was to come.

However, my brave thoughts dwindled the following day when I went back to the remains of our plant. Alex, our foreman, Mike and our son were sorting through the debris. They were salvaging charred boxes of remanufactured parts. Later, they would be opened, the parts inspected and tested. "If they're good," said Mike, "we're just that much ahead in starting anew."

"It's one thing we can do now," he added.

*This one thing I do...*those words echoed in my mind: from Paul's letter to the Philippians (3:13) "...but this one thing I do, forgetting those things which are behind, and reaching forth unto those things which are before."

I walked over to some blackened boxes, picked one up and pulled away the cardboard to expose the power cylinder in its protective plastic wrapper. I unwrapped it, and the part looked fine.

And we salvaged one part after another. I was heartened to find that a number of them appeared untouched. Testing later proved their perfect condition. By noon I had salvaged a number of parts and found I also had salvaged my optimism. I walked over to Mike and put my arm around his waist. "You're right, Honey," I said, "there's no reason why we can't start over!"

It was the old lesson. Putting one's hands to work is the best antidote for morosity. "The devil finds work for idle hands to do." And he also finds it for idle minds. Most often, the "work" he supplies is despondency and hopelessness. Yes, keeping busy and looking forward is the best antidote to hopelessness.

For days all of us picked through the wreckage, salvaging what we could. And as I did, I found myself wondering about God's role in all this.

Then one of our Sunday school students asked, "How could God allow such a thing to happen to you?" I had my answer.

"No, Honey," I said, "God didn't 'allow' the fire to happen. Nor does He 'allow' people to die in train wrecks or cars to crash into each other. It's usually humans that cause these tragedies. Just as someone carelessly left greasy overalls on an electric heater that caused our place to burn down, so does careless driving and other human error cause accidents.

"Where is God in all this?" I continued. "Look in Romans 8:28. Put the tragedy in His hands, and let Him work out the good."

And that's what happened with us. Remember when Michael Jr. spoke about our need for more space? That was a week or so before the fire. In the meantime he had been scouting around and located a larger building not far away from our Fifth Street location. It was at 121 Clearfield Street.

Of course, it was the perfect answer. We were able to get a lease on it. But only half of our problem was solved. What were we going to do for work benches on which to set up our assembly line? Such equipment costs money, and our finances were limited. How long would our little company be out of business? Every non-productive day drove us closer to bankruptcy.

"Well," said Mike as we got out of the car in front of the new building, "all we can do is keep walking in faith."

"Yes," added Michael Jr., "just one step at a time."

Mike pushed open the door of the low building, reached in and turned on the lights. As the overhead fluorescents blazed, I gasped. Strewn all over the floor were big barrels and packing cases. The lease specified that the premises be clean. This place was a mess.

I turned to my husband. "Mike, we'd better get on the phone to the landlord right now!"

He took my arm. "Only if we want to thank him," he sighed happily. Was he out of his mind? I looked at my son. He, too, had that same pleased look.

What was going on?

Mike pointed it out to me. "You see those drums and cases? Well, they're just waist high. All we have to do is get some boards and we've got our benches."

Already, Michael Jr., along with some employees, was heading to the lumberyard. Within hours, planks were laid across the boxes and barrels, and only three days after the fire, A-1 Remanufactured products were coming off the assembly line again.

Again and again God has proven Romans 8:28 to me. Mike called late one day to say he was bringing home a very important business prospect for dinner. They'd be home within an hour!

"Mike," I exclaimed, "you've got to be kidding! You know we're painting the dining room. We have no place to eat."

"Oh, the kitchen should be all right," he said.

"But, Mike," I pressed, "I have nothing to serve him. All I have is that cabbage and macaroni dish. And that's nothing to give a guest!" This was a simple macaroni dish I made of cabbage, oil, garlic and macaroni.

"Oh, you'll find something, Fran," he said. "Gotta go, good-bye." Click went the phone. I sat there staring at the wall in frustration. *What are you going to do with a man like that?* I wondered. Then I started praying. *Father, this is desperate. Please help.*

Scurrying around, I found one small steak in the refrigerator. *Maybe it will do,* I thought. I put the steak under the burner and set up the kitchen table for three. No sooner was the steak done when Mike and the business prospect came into the front door.

He was a nice-looking man, evidently very prosperous and used to finer things. How would he feel about eating in the kitchen?

"I'm so sorry," I apologized, "but our dining room is being painted. Do you mind eating in our kitchen?"

"Kitchen?" he exclaimed, his eyes lighting up. "Wonderful!" We walked into the kitchen, and he slid behind the table. "You know, when I was a boy," he said, "I used to always eat in the kitchen when I visited my grandmother's. It was my favorite place. But in our own home?" He shook his head sadly. "Mother always made the family eat in the dining room, and I never felt comfortable there. It was so cold and formal. But here? I feel good again." He took a deep breath and sighed in satisfaction. "This is like being at Grandma's again."

We gave thanks to the Lord for our food, then I got up, got the steak out of the oven and set it before him. But he had his eyes focused on the bowl of cabbage at the other end of the table.

"What's that?" he asked.

"Oh, a little cabbage dish I make," I said. "You might not like it."

"Hmmm, smells good," he said. "Let me try some."

I spooned a little on his plate.

He ate it with relish. "Wow!" he exclaimed, "that's wonderful! I've never tasted anything that good before. Can I have some more?"

By the time dinner was over he had finished three platefuls.

The next morning a delivery man rang the doorbell with a big bouquet of roses. It was from the business prospect. The card read: *To the woman who made me feel like a little boy again.*

Needless to say, the business arrangement he and Mike put together was very successful. After that Mike jokingly suggested he bring all his important prospects home for my cabbage, garlic and pasta dinners.

"But let's get the dining room painted first," I said. "Not all your prospects will have the same kind of grandmother."

Ever since then I have called that particular cabbage

dish my Romans 8:28 recipe.

Our company grew, and as it expanded more people came to help us. Jacquie, Michael's wife was now helping do our books. As in our old location, I still found myself relating closely with the women employees. We'd all eat our lunches together, taking sandwiches out of brown paper bags, using packing cases as tables and chairs. When I first joined the group, one of the women jumped up, pulled a chair from behind a desk and held it for me. "Sit down *here*, Mrs. Cardone," she said.

I waved it away. "Thank you so much, Marie," I said, sitting on a packing case, "but this will do me nicely."

Perhaps this is why we developed such a close rapport with our employees. One of the secrets of getting along with people, whether they be employees, friends, acquaintances or family members, is to treat everyone equally and fairly; you'll make loyal friends.

I'll never forget how this worked out with Lydia Kasakov, the little Brazilian lady I helped get started working with us. As I mentioned, she had become quite proficient in her work and was a veritable computer with catalog part numbers.

One day Mike asked me to go to the bank to handle some papers. So I dressed up in my good clothes and afterward stopped back at the plant. As I was talking with the women, one of our new employees, Tony, a rough, outspoken man who didn't know my experience with the company, happened to come into the office to pick up some worksheets. Seeing me all dressed up, he winked at the other women and said loudly: "Hey, Mrs.

Cardone, I betcha you can't do *their kind* of work!"

At this Lydia jumped up. Placing herself before him, hands on hips, she stamped her foot and shouted, "What you think? Missas Cardone teaches *me* this work! She *teaches* me!"

Tony stared open-mouthed at her, not knowing what had hit him, then he quickly backed out of the room, hands up in admitted defeat.

Lydia turned to me and winked.The whole group of women exploded into laughter. From then on, whenever Tony came into the office, he was very meek. Thinking of Lydia's outburst reminded me of how angry Jesus got when He chased the money-changers out of the temple. I guess there's a time and place for a little righteous indignation!

Cardone Industries continued to expand, and more and more employees were hired. I was always amazed at the criteria by which my husband hired people. Often he'd put someone on a job for which I felt the person unsuited. Surprisingly, after a few months the man or woman would turn out to be just right in that capacity.

I mentioned this to Mike one evening at supper.

"Well," he said leaning forward, "I believe God has blessed each of us with a special talent to use for His good in the world. Sometimes we get sidetracked along the way, and not until later do we discover what we really want to do.

"Look at the author A.J. Cronin," he said. "He became a doctor, yet all the while he had this calling within him to be a writer. And today we have his beautiful books, such as *Keys of the Kingdom,* which has done much to advance the cause of God."

He sat back in his chair and smiled. "I was expected to be a coal miner back in Hughestown." He looked down at himself and laughed: "How long do you think I would have lasted in *that* job?" he chuckled. Then he added quietly, "It was a job which broke the health of my father, who was a big, sturdy man.

"No, Fran," he continued, "getting back to your comment about the right job for the person, we often give new people a succession of different jobs, let them try out various assignments. Usually, both they and we can tell which one best suits them. That's what makes for happiness in one's work—doing the thing you were created to do."

As Mike talked I thought of all the people who had found their true calling with us. There was Tony Lombardi, a barber, who became a crackerjack core buyer. Then there was Mark Spuler, now our executive vice president, who had studied to be a sociologist. And there was Allan Giordano, who sold potato chips on a retail store delivery route. Now he's our executive vice president/planning.

The great spiritual writer Oswald Chambers had something to say about God's calling on our lives. He wrote about it in *My Utmost for His Highest*. I'll try to paraphrase it:

> The call of God is not the echo of my nature. My personal affinities and temperament are not considered. As long as I listen to my own personal wishes and temperament and decide what I am fitted for, I shall never hear the call of God. But when I am brought into close

relationship with Him, I am in the same condition the prophet Isaiah was in. Isaiah's soul was so in tune with God by the tremendous crisis he had gone through that he heard God loud and clear. The majority of us have no ear for anything but ourselves, and so we cannot hear a thing God says. But when we're brought into that zone where we hear the call of God, we are profoundly altered."

Now some people say we should not compare God's calling with such mundane things as the work we do in this world. To me that's ridiculous. I believe God puts us into this world not only to help spread the gospel but to help our fellowmen through our work.

I saw this in our own family. Sometime ago I read a theory by a Christian psychologist who believed that whatever a child is good at in his younger years is an indication of the profession in which he will excel. For example, if a child shows a proficiency in art, he may well be suited for a career in graphics, such as an illustrator or a fashion designer.

There was no question about Michael Jr.'s talent. Not only did he take to mechanics like a duck to water, but he maintained his interest all through his growing-up years. His own automobile hardly saw a garage. If a repair was needed, he'd fix it. One morning he had worked long and hard on his car. When I went out to see how he was doing, he emerged from under the hood, his face and hands as black as the coal his grandfather used to mine. Eyes shining, he proclaimed: "Fixed it, Mom."

"How did you do it?" I asked.

"With a spoke from the wheel of my bicycle," he said.

Naturally, Michael's talent stood him in good stead when he began helping his father run the plant. But as our business grew and new developments came along, some friction developed between father and son.

[1] And we know that all that happens to us is working for our good if we love God and are fitting into His plans. (TLB)

This Is My Story This Is My Song

Chapter Fourteen

FACING THE FUTURE

I don't know what to do about him, Fran," sighed Mike one evening as we sat in our living room. I knew he was talking about our son. Michael Jr. who had been on board a few years now and was now coming up with some new ideas. It was understandable. He had not only studied the latest business methods at the university but had kept up-to-date with the amazing progress of the computer world. He was so excited about it.

"Mom, it's mind-boggling what computers can do," he told me at lunch one day. "They can handle everything from inventory control to quality control on the assembly line."

My husband wasn't so sure. And I could see his side

of it too. He had started out rebuilding vacuum windshield wiper motors fresh out of high school. His tools were pliers, screwdriver and a hammer. When he started his own company, inventory control was keeping a good eye count. In Mike's view our plant was going along well enough without automation.

I could also see signs of growing dissension between father and son, arguments behind closed office doors, spirited discussions from which my husband would turn away shaking his head. I found myself in the middle trying to keep peace. That evening in our living room when the subject came up, I could tell Mike was really suffering. "All these new ideas and changing things," he mused. "I find it difficult to understand them."

I looked up from my sewing. "I know what you mean," I said, biting off a thread. "But we have to remember, Mike, the world is changing, and we have to change along with it. Ruth tells me her children are learning about computers in grade school today. When you and I went to school, we did our figures with pencil on a yellow-lined pad, remember?"

"I know, I know," sighed Mike, picking up his newspaper. "But I guess I'm like an old dog who finds it difficult to learn new tricks."

A few days later while visiting at Michael's house, I took him aside. "Please don't push your father so hard," I said. "He knows you mean well. But you must remember, he founded one business, then started another. It isn't easy for him to jump right into something entirely new." I patted him on the shoulder. "Your father loves you, Michael. Be patient and give him a little time."

Back and forth I went trying to sow seeds of peace. As in all family disagreements, I had learned one person can be a mediator if he or she can bring a little sugar to each side.

Finally both of them began to see the other's point of view. Michael Jr. became more patient and took more time to explain his recommendations, showing how they could benefit. In turn, Mike set aside his prejudices against automation and started listening.

In the end, new automated controls, electronic data processing and other computerized systems were put to work. Their worth was soon proven in increased assembly-line efficiencies, improved inventory control and order filling.

In a way, I felt a part of it all. "Blessed are the peacemakers," Jesus said in His Sermon on the Mount (Matt. 5:9). And I truly felt blessed.

After Mike and our son had settled their differences, he and I were talking about how well the new systems in the plant were working out. Mike leaned back in his chair and said, "Well, if Michael had come out of college not knowing anything more than I, I guess you'd have to say his school was a total loss." Then he winked at me and added, "Just between you and me, Fran, I'll never become accustomed to those crazy computers."

I got up and patted him on the shoulder. "That's OK," I laughed, "just as long as we have folks who know how to use them."

As our daughter, Ruthie, said, our grandchildren were already becoming familiar with computers. By the time they entered the business world, they would be as familiar with them as our generation was with the adding machine.

In fact, by 1978 some of our grandchildren were already working at Cardone Industries. One day while I was walking through the plant with some worksheets, Mike took my arm. "Come," he said quietly, "I want to show you something." He led me over to the area where our cores were received. These heavy, grimy metal units such as brake cylinders, power-steering units and blower motors are usually delivered from the outside in barrels. Mike pointed to two young boys, black with grease, eagerly emptying the barrels and sorting out the cores. I took another look and gasped. They were Ruth's sons, Eric, age nine and Roger, age eight.

"They're faster at that job than most of the men," said Mike. I looked at him. He was beaming with pride, and I could see that his long-held dream of seeing his son follow him in the business had expanded to include his grandchildren. "But so young..." I was about to say, then caught myself, remembering Michael going to St. Louis to take the Carter Carburetor course when he was fourteen and, at about the same time, graduating from General Motors' tune-up and carburization course, the youngest ever to do this.

I looked at Eric and Roger, and I knew what my husband was thinking: "Teach a child to choose the right path, and when he is older he will remain upon it" (Prov. 22:6, TLB).

They were adding more than earning money for their savings account, I thought. They were also learning the ways of the world. They knew we had promised God to be completely fair in all our dealings.

But they were also discovering not everyone believed in the same principles. For example, they found out that once in a while someone would try to get a ten-dollar rebate for a core worth only one dollar. And, as the Bible advises, they realized that though one must have the heart of a dove, one must also see with the eye of the serpent.

Ruthie and I were discussing this one afternoon at our house. Thank goodness she lived nearby so we could get together often. "The way it looks, Ma," she said, "our whole family is going to be in the remanufacturing business. Even little Patricia says she's looking forward to the time when she can work in the office." We were preparing dinner for a big family get-together that night.

Ruthie was so much more than a daughter to me, she was a close friend, one in whom I could confide and one in whom I could always find support. We shared the same love of music. For years I had played the organ at Calvary Temple and now Ruth had been filling in for me when we were away.

One of our greatest joys was playing the piano and organ together at our house, Ruth at the piano as I played the organ or vice versa. We sang favorite old hymns such as *In Times Like These, For He Is So Precious To Me* and *My Faith Looks Up To Thee.*

One afternoon I'll never forget. A cold rain was falling; we had just finished one hymn. It was quiet in the house except for the rain hissing at the windows. Slowly Ruth started the chords of a hymn. I didn't recognize it at first, but as she continued I recognized it as *Where the Roses Never Fade.* For some reason I sat still at the organ, unable to accompany here, a strange mixture of emotions coursing through me, my heart full of gratitude for a loving daughter so close to me, and a mystical feeling about that song that transcended both space and time.

Her eyes were closed as she played, then as the last note hung in the air, she opened them and laughed. "Forgive me, Ma, I think I got carried away."

I got up and walked over to the piano, gave her a big hug and held her for a long moment, then forcing a laugh, said: "c'mon, let's go see about that macaroni."

Much of the talk at the table that night was about business, of course, since so much of the family was involved in Cardone Industries. As we talked over old times, there was much to laugh about. Turning to Mike, I said: "Remember that letter I wrote for you to a sales rep, George Rayburn, way back when we first got started?"

Mike chuckled. "Yes, the one you wrote by hand, and he said, 'What kind of company sends out handwritten letters?'"

"And then," I continued, "later on after he came to work for us, he sent *you* a handwritten letter, and that's when I got back at him."

"Yes," grinned Mike. "I remember it well. It was at a salesmen's banquet, and you mentioned his letter before the group, saying: 'What kind of salesman is it who writes his letters in long hand?' and everybody broke up laughing."

"And it was George Rayburn himself who laughed the loudest," I added, thinking how good it was talking over old memories.

But there were always new things to talk about too. New factories were continually being established as our lines and production increased. That meant my signing papers along with my husband with each new acquisition.

While at the table I told the family that the only way I learned when my husband and Michael were about to acquire a new property was when our lawyer called me and asked, "Frances, what is your husband up to now?"

To us, the most important phase of each new plant addition was its dedication. These services would be presided over by well-known religious leaders, such as Oral Roberts, Rex Humbard, Norman Vincent Peale and Charles Stanley, who would dedicate the new plant to our Four Corporate Goals:

1. Honor God in all we do.
2. Help people develop.
3. Pursue excellence.
4. Grow profitably.

These principles hold true, and Cardone Industries prospered. As busy years passed, there was continuing expansion in our family too. In 1973 Michael announced that Jacquie would not be helping out much longer in the office. They were expecting their first child. Little Michael Cardone III was born on February 19, 1974. Unlike his father's difficult entry into the world, his birth was trouble-free, for which I thanked God. As I looked at the little one asleep on his first day in this world and wondered about his destiny, I thought back to his grandfather and father and how no one could tell at their births what their futures held. My husband, born in a small hamlet, seemed destined to work in a coal mine. When our son entered the world, there was no future for him in his father's company. What would this new little one's future be? I wondered. Whatever it was, it was completely in God's hands. And so I prayed that he would follow the Proverb that had guided all the Cardones: "Trust in the Lord with all thine heart; and lean not unto thine own understanding. In all thy ways acknowledge him, and he shall direct thy paths " (3:5-6).

If he followed these precepts he could not go wrong.

In the meantime, Mike's mother passed on. She had lived a good, holy life, and as we gathered for her funeral, I felt the camaraderie of all Mike's brothers and sisters. I thanked God that our friendships had been maintained. Nothing would make his mother happier as she looked down from heaven at us.

Our son's family continued to grow. Beautiful little Christin was born July 21, 1976, and Ryan came along three years later. Ryan was a miracle baby in every sense of the word. He was born with spina bifida, which not only threatened his life, but promised to cripple him so that he would never walk. Hundreds of people prayed for little Ryan, and what appeared to be irreversible damage was miraculously healed through the power of the Holy Spirit. Within a few years Ryan was running like any other little boy. While worrying about Ryan, I had not been feeling well myself. In fact, for almost a year I knew I had a problem, but like too many of us I felt if I ignored it, it would go away. As I know that God heals, I also believe He uses doctors and medicine to accomplish His purposes. Now I realized I was wrong in not seeing a doctor sooner.

Only when I began to hemorrhage did I make an emergency appointment with my doctor. After examining me, he said: "Mrs. Cardone, I'm going to have you admitted to the hospital immediately."

How one's plans can change in the blink of an eye! That evening I had been planning a dinner to celebrate the opening of our grandson Eric's carburetor rebuilding business. I couldn't believe it; it seemed only yesterday that Eric was a toddler. Now he was a young man. His father, Ruben Tarno, Ruth's husband, now owned his own rebuilding company, which my husband helped him get started. Eric was following in his father's footsteps, just as Roger would do later.

So instead of hosting a dinner, I was in the hospital having emergency surgery. My doctor's face was grave as he sat down beside my bed after the operation.

"Well?" I asked fearfully, "is it malignant?"

"It might be," he said. That Bible verse seemed to ring in my head: "The thing which I greatly feared is come upon me" (Job 3:25).

"What are we going to do about it?" I choked.

He said I would be given radiation treatments.

"What then?"

"We'll have to face that when we come to it."

When he left the room, I turned my face to the wall and sobbed. I heard a step and turned to see a man coming through the door. It was Jack Hecker, a business friend of ours. "I'll only be a minute," he said, "I wanted to give this to you."

He was a Gideon, and he handed me a little red Bible. I was very grateful. In the rush of going to the hospital, I had left mine at home. I grasped it as if it were the most precious thing on earth. "Thank you," I whispered. He smiled and left. A little later my son and husband came in; both were crying. I could only put my arms around each of them and try to comfort them.

After they left, the room was quiet. As I lay there, a cold, deadly fear of what might happen began to fill me. Terror, like an evil spirit lurking in the shadows of the room, leaped onto me, and I cried out. Feeling desperately alone, I started to ring for the nurse when my hand brushed up against something on my bed. It was the little red Bible Mr. Hecker had brought.

I picked it up, and it fell open to Psalm 16. The first verse of that chapter seemed to leap off the page: *"Preserve me, O God: for in Thee do I put my trust."*

As I read those words I was filled with a strong sense of His presence. For in those words I recognized a binding covenant between God and myself.

Preserve me, O God was His part of the covenant.

...for in thee do I put my trust was my part.

It was that clear; He would preserve me if I put my trust in Him.

Lord Jesus, I prayed, *You have my trust, completely and unequivocally.*

In committing my illness to Him, I felt a new confidence surge through me. *David must have felt the same confidence,* I thought, *when he wrote that Psalm.* I pictured him hiding in the wilderness knowing a powerful enemy, the vengeful Saul, was out to kill him. He had no one to turn to but his God; his complete trust in the Lord delivered him.

I, too, was now trembling in the wilderness, fearful of a powerful and evil malignancy out to destroy me.

And I, too, had no one to turn to but my God. So again and again I affirmed His healing by repeating those twelve vital words.

When my son and husband returned, they found a more composed woman. As I told them the source of my help, I could see their shoulders sag in relief. What grieved me now was seeing the pain in Ruthie when she came to visit. Laying her tear-stained face on my breast, she sobbed: "Oh, Ma, I feel so bad with you in here like this! I wish I could help you in some way."

"Ruthie," I soothed, stroking her head, "I have all the help I need." And I told her about my covenant.

I needed it desperately. For five long weeks I went to the oncological cancer research center for daily radiation treatments. All through them I prayed my affirmation, believing it as much as I believed the sun was coming up the next morning.

Then came my most trying ordeal. For four excruciating days with radium pellets inserted within me I had to lie flat on my back, not moving a muscle. Again, I breathed: *Preserve me, O God: for in thee do I put my trust.*

A month passed before a second surgery could be scheduled. Most nerve-wracking was the waiting. Finally, in October 1979, I was back in the hospital. As I was wheeled down corridors watching the ceiling panels and light fixtures move past, I prayed my promise and commitment.

The last thing I remember before going under the anesthesia was my murmuring: *Preserve me, O God....*

Then I was awake with the faces of my family and doctor grouped around me, all smiling.

"Congratulations, Mrs. Cardone," my doctor said. "We found everything in order. Not a trace of the cancer could be found."

"Praise God," I breathed, squeezing my loved ones' hands. He had preserved me.

I have done a lot of thinking about that verse since then. I know my prayer made me feel better and gave me confidence. But did it really affect the cancer?

Let me tell you about a medical report I read in the *Southern Medical Journal* by Randolph C. Byrd, a medical doctor in San Francisco. He wanted to evaluate the effects of intercessory prayer on a group of seriously ill heart patients. Out of a group of 939 patients, half consented to having prayers said for them by born-again Christians, the other half did not. What happened? The "prayer" group had an overall better outcome and had fewer requirements for antibiotics, diuretics and intubation/ventilation, according to Dr. Byrd.

But I did not need a medical report to know that prayer *works*.

Ever since I have carried that verse with me. When a friend went into the hospital for a heart operation, I printed it on a large card and taped it to her wall so she could easily read it from her bed.

After she recovered, she told me how much her "little covenant" helped her. I have since given it to many friends, who have also attested to its help.

The one to whom I never dreamed I would be giving it was my daughter, Ruth.

Chapter Fifteen

MY DAUGHTER, MY FRIEND

ometimes I find myself wondering, Did Satan go
to God and, as with Job, point down at my
husband and me and say: "Take something
precious from those two and *then* see how loyal they are
to You"?

My husband and I had been talking about starting a
church in our area for local people. But we had
absolutely no idea of the tragedy that was coming our
way. The years had been good. Cardone Industries had
grown to twenty plants and some two thousand
employees to become the largest privately-held
remanufacturer of auto parts in the world. Michael had
taken over the reins of the company as president. My
husband was chairman of the board and, though less

active on the scene, was still very much involved. So was I. Whenever our phone rang at home, bringing news of a problem at the plant, and Mike would discuss it, I would go to our other phone, lay hands on it and pray for the situation.

But in 1989 I found myself praying desperately for someone near and dear to me, our forty-seven-year-old daughter Ruth. We were not only mother and daughter but close friends. She had been visiting us in Florida that Christmas. When she got off the plane she looked pale.

Oh, well, I thought, blaming the Philadelphia winter, *a few days in the sun will have her glowing.* However, she wasn't that interested in the beach, and I noticed a lassitude about her.

One morning at breakfast she asked, "Ma, do you have any vitamins?"

"Why?" I responded. She had never taken them before.

"Oh, I...I just haven't been feeling well lately."

I leaned forward and took her hand. "Honey, I don't like the way you look. Please, for your family's sake, see a doctor."

However, Ruthie was not one to run to a doctor, but when she found a lump in her breast while showering, she did.

"Ma," her voiced quavered on the phone, "it's cancer."

I gripped the phone, silently crying, "No, God, no, not my Ruthie!"

She bravely tried to cheer me. "Ma, it's not as bad as it seems. They're going to give me chemotherapy, and the doctors are hopeful."

It all happened so fast. She had a mastectomy. I stayed with her through the surgery, and when she was conscious I held her in my arms. "Ma," she sobbed, "I feel so ugly."

"No, my darling," I soothed, "you're as beautiful as ever." Her husband, Ruben stayed close by her side trying to cheer her up, telling her how great their sons, Roger and Eric, were doing in their own businesses. Little ten-year-old Patricia, their daughter, a blessing who came late in their marriage, clung to her mother. Patricia truly was a gift from God. In her I could see a discernment far beyond her years. She seemed to understand what Jesus told us: *"Here on earth you will have many trials and sorrows"* (John 16:33, TLB). However, I, her grandmother, still had trouble accepting this.

Then, miraculously, Ruthie began to feel better. Was this a remission that would last? I prayed, oh, how I prayed. In a few months it seemed like old times again. In fact, Ruthie was excited about her and Ruben's upcoming silver anniversary.

"Can you believe it, Ma, twenty-five years?" she bubbled. She sat across the table from me as we were having lunch at my house. "Why, it seems only yesterday I was working in the office and Ruben was bringing me coffee." She looked into the distance with a thoughtful smile. "That was his way of courting me, and *you* knew it all the time." She laughed. But as I studied her wan face, my heart went out to her. Despite her bright spirit, the ravages of pain were visible, and she was so thin. The hand that squeezed mine was almost paralyzed from her illness.

She wanted us to play the organ and piano together as we had through the years. But after sitting down at the piano and trying a few chords, she shook her head. "I'm sorry, but these fingers just don't work the way they used to."

She brightened as she told me about her plans for her and Ruben's anniversary party. "It will be at the Melrose Country Club," she said, "and I've already worked out the decorating scheme. There will be flowers on each table with tiny silver lights, the tables will be covered in silver cloths and so will the backs of the chair. And then the next day we're off on our cruise to the Bahamas!"

She was so excited, and I was happy to see a flush fill her hollow cheeks.

On the night of their anniversary party she looked radiant. The consummate hostess, she circulated among the silver-topped tables, greeting friends and family members. Among the guests were childhood friends.

However, I should have realized it was like the bright flare of a light bulb just before it burns out. For on the day she returned from their anniversary cruise she went right to the hospital.

At her bedside I reminded her of the covenant verse: *Preserve me, O God: for in thee do I put my trust"* (Ps. 16:1).

"Yes, I know it, Ma," said Ruthie, her brown eyes full of pain, her skin so translucent the veins showed through. "I'm holding on to it."

Later, Mike and I talked to her doctor. "What do you see?" I asked. He studied my daughter's charts on his desk and slowly shook his head. Looking up at us, he said: "The cancer has gone to her liver. I don't see any hope."

I sat dumbfounded. To have the prognosis stated so irrevocably made my blood run cold.

"My feeling is," he added, "that you should let your daughter go home where she'll be in familiar surroundings."

You mean let her die at home, I thought, not wanting to accept the thought. I tried to stand, but my legs were wobbly. Mike helped me to my feet. There seemed nothing else to do. A hospital bed was brought to my daughter's house and set up in their bedroom. A nurse to attend her was arranged for.

I prayed that Ruth would be comfortable. At first she seemed well enough to worry about the hospital bed hurting their rug. "Ma, don't you think the weight and rollers will crush the carpeting?"

I patted her hand. "No, Honey," I assured her, "not one bit." As I watched the stricken faces of her husband, sons and daughter, I knew that Ruben would pay for a million rugs if he could only have his wife back.

As weeks passed Ruthie sank lower and lower. She knew she was leaving us. As she told a close friend, "I'm not afraid to die; God will take care of my children." She smiled wanly at her friend. "I will see you in heaven." At Christmas Ruben carried her downstairs where she sat among us in a wheelchair. We sang carols and hymns together and distributed gifts. Her eyes glistened as she admired the Christmas tree her children had decorated, and I wondered what this home would be like the next time those ornaments were unpacked.

On New Year's Day she couldn't come down at all. On January 10, we all sat in Ruth's room with her. Hardly any of us spoke for fear of disturbing her; her frail form looked so small in that bed. Then her nurse, in a moment of inspiration which I'll always appreciate, put a cassette in a tape player and turned it on. It was an evangelist singing that old-time gospel hymn "Where the Roses Never Fade"—one of Ruthie's favorites.

As the music filled the room, I noticed Ruth's pale white hand began moving up and down to the rhythm. Softly at first, but gaining in spirit, Ruth began singing along with the hymn...

I am going to a city where the streets with gold are laid

Where the tree of life is blooming, and the roses never fade.

Here they bloom but for a season, soon their beauty is decayed

I am going to a city, where the roses never fade.

I began singing along with her, and then my heart almost stopped. I remembered a time a year earlier when we had sung that hymn together in my living room and a mystical feeling had come over me. My voice broke; I couldn't sing anymore.

But Ruth's faint, ethereal voice kept singing...

In this world we have our troubles, Satan's snares we must evade

We'll be free from all temptations, where the roses never fade.

Loved ones gone to be with Jesus, in their robes of white arrayed

Now are waiting for my coming, where the roses never fade.

Out of tear-dimmed eyes I caught a movement in the room and saw that her daughter, Patricia, had gotten her little toy tape recorder and was recording her mother's last hymn.

On the night of January 9, Ruth's frail voice gave out, and she could not sing anymore. She stared up at the ceiling and gasped, "I've had it...."

Ruben leaned over her, tears streaming down his face. Looking up at him, she managed a smile, "We had a good twenty-five years," she said, "a wonderful life together." Then I leaned down and put my arms around her. She whispered, "There's nobody like your mother."

Mike told her quietly, "Don't worry, Ruthie, we'll all be here to take care of your kids."

The next morning word came. "Her doctor fears she won't last the day."

We rushed over and sat at her bedside, her husband, children, Michael and Jacquie, Mike and I, praying for her. Slower and slower her bosom rose and fell, and at three o'clock in the afternoon she gasped and was gone.

My impulse was to run screaming out of the house, but I sensed strong arms holding me, comforting me. I thought it was my husband, but glancing up I saw him sitting, shoulders heaving, face buried in his hands. I knew then it was the Lord who held me. I could only sigh through my tears: "Lord, I still love You."

Losing my daughter, my friend, was a tragedy I believed I could never face. People are supposed to bury their parents, not their children. The days following were a blur. Numbed with grief, I moved mechanically among the thousands of mourners at the funeral. Those giving eulogies were Richard Roberts, son of Oral Roberts, and Judge Joseph Bruno of Philadelphia, an old family friend.

In his talk Judge Bruno said, "Ruthie had a way of making you feel good. I'll always remember her coming up to me and saying, 'Oh, Judge, I love your tie,'" He stopped for a moment and wiped his eyes. "When I get to heaven I know she's going to come up to me and say, 'Oh, Joe, I love your tie.'"

So many people came up to me to say such things as "You don't know me, but I loved your daughter. Every time she saw me walking to the store she'd pick me up in her car."

Ruthie's favorite hymns were sung, including "What a Friend We Have in Jesus" and "For He Is So Precious to Me." She was buried in Sunrise Cemetery.

Riding home, I happened to notice through the limousine window a street vagrant in filthy clothes, shuffling along, drinking from a bottle in a paper bag. Anger flooded me. *Why does God take the good ones and let the bad ones go on living?* And then I realized how wrong I was, and I remembered the Lord telling us in Isaiah 55:8, *"My thoughts are not your thoughts, neither are your ways my ways."*

In days following I found myself continually praying for His presence to sustain me, to fill the empty void within me. I knew I would never know in this life why a loving God would take my daughter. But I did seek an answer for my pain. And as I studied His Word, again going over Jesus' message, *"Here on earth you will have many trials and sorrows,"* I realized that pain

*and death in this life are inevitable. Instead of denying
it, we must accept it. As Tim Hansel, author of* You
Gotta Keep Dancin', put it so well: "Pain is inevitable,
but misery is optional." Shawn Strannigan, another gift
writer, who had lost a young child, explained it in a way
that really helped me. "I realized that suffering is a
natural consequence of living," he wrote, "and the
harder we resist pain, the more intense it will be."

And so slowly I began to accept my pain, and in the
very acceptance of it I felt His comfort. In looking up to
God, I realized He is in charge, He has the last say about
things and it isn't ours to ask why—just to accept. And
so, despite what may happen, I trust Him, knowing He
loves us and is concerned for our good.

In walking through the fire I found myself growing.
As Job told us in 23:10, "When he has tested me, I will
come forth as gold" (NKJV).

And He did test me. Ten days after Ruthie left us,
my mother died of a stroke at the age of ninety. Again I
grieved, but I was already being sustained by the
strength I had been given after Ruth's death, strength I
knew would sustain me through whatever the future
would bring.

Though Ruth was close to my mother and had
visited her often, we did not tell my mother of her death,
as we felt it would be better to wait a bit. This resulted
in one of those bright touches that God seems to give us
at a time when we need it most.

As we talked over lunch about my mother's not
knowing Ruthie had died, our grandson, Roger, stopped
eating and said, "I can just see it when they meet in
heaven. Mom will say, 'Gramma, what are *you* doing

here?' And Gramma will look at Mom and say: 'Whatcha *you-a-doin'* here? Go back-a-home to your kids!'"

We all laughed. How true is that old proverb: *"a merry heart doeth good"* (Prov. 17:22); I felt sure Ruth and Mom were laughing along with us.

It was around that same kitchen table a few days later that I believe God in His mysterious way gave us another healing illumination. Mike and I were at lunch, both of us lost in our thoughts, the room quiet except for a January wind which moaned at the windows and scattered dead leaves in the yard.

Suddenly Mike looked up and said, "Maybe God took Ruthie away to save her from some terrible thing that might have happened to her later in life, a bad accident or other tragedy."

Before I had a chance to answer, the phone rang. I picked it up to hear our son, Michael, exclaim, "Mom, I've just been given a revelation. God must have taken Ruthie to keep her from going through some awful experience later in her life."

I was stunned by this confirmation. Before I could even speak, Michael went on. "For some reason I was led to this Scripture on this, Isaiah 57:1. Here, let me read it to you from *The Living Bible: "The good men perish; the godly die before their time...No one seems to realize that God is taking them away from evil days ahead."*

"What do you think, Mom?" he asked. It was all too much for me, and I had to sink into a chair.

Finally I found my voice and told him what his father and I had just been discussing. "Isn't that something?" he said. "Well, I don't know what it all really means, Mom, but I've got to tell you I get a lot of comfort out of it. Take care. I've got to get back to work."

He hung up, and I turned to Mike, who had deduced what Michael had told me from our conversation.

"I can't believe it," he said, shaking his head in wonderment. "We got the same thought too?"

"Yes," I said, pondering it all. What could happen in the future that would hurt Ruth so? I wondered. Then I realized it was not for us to know. Perhaps one day we'll be shown, perhaps not. But again I accepted it as one more little illumination that helped us through her loss.

Accepting the loss of a loved one is one thing. But to gain something through it? Before Ruth's death I would not have believed this. But I have found that Romans 8:28—"...*we know that all that happens to us is working for our good if we love God and are fitting into His plans*"—can even apply to our most tragic losses.

For something good has come out of it. With Ruthie with the Lord, I feel heaven is so much closer to me now. It is as when your child goes to work in a foreign country. You want to find out all you can about that country; it has so much more personal meaning to you.

Moreover, I am finding that I now have a new ministry helping others who suffer as I have. For when you have walked through the fire, you can help heal others who have been seared. As writer Shawn Strannigan says, "It's much easier to help bind the wounded when you have scars of your own."

Before, I was timid about approaching someone

who had lost a loved one. I wasn't sure what to say and was afraid I might be clumsy and intrusive. Now when I hear of a person who is bereaved, I contact them right away to let them know I share their grief and understand their sorrow.

My experience seems to have given me the right words to say or, in certain cases, the wisdom not to say a thing. This happened after I walked up to the door of a woman who had lost two sons in their twenties in an accident. She met me at the door, her face lined with grief. She knew I had been through the same fire. There was no talking between us, no need for it. We embraced, and in that unspoken fellowship of shared sorrow, healing came.

I visited another mother mourning her little girl, who had been struck by a car outside her house. She couldn't understand why God would allow such a thing to happen. I assured her God did not want her daughter to die, that it was the evil of this world in the form of an intoxicated motorist. And I was able to help her find God's presence in sustaining her through her grief.

"Lord, I know You have a reason for it," is all one who has suffered can say. The only peace we can find in sorrow is knowing God knows what He is doing. God never promised us a happy life. His Son told us, *"In this world you will have trouble"* (John 16:33, NIV). But He does promise us His unfailing love, His healing peace, His enduring faithfulness to see us through the terrible times that strike us all.

In the end we must remember that God allowed His only Son to suffer a horrifying death on the cross for our sake. Can there be any greater love?

From my own experience I have also learned there is a right and a wrong way to talk with a grieving person. After Ruth died, would-be sympathizers came up to me and said, "You can be happy that Ruth is with the Lord now." Well-meaning as those words may be, they are simply platitudes. I *know* Ruth is with the Lord and that she is happy. But *I* still hurt deeply. I especially miss her friendship.

What helped me most was when a thoughtful person would say, "Oh, Frances, we know Ruth is with the Lord, but we also know how deeply you hurt over her loss." Yes, I do hurt, and I know I will suffer for a long time. It helps to have others acknowledge this. One person staggering under the weight of a coffin is excruciating, but when five others help carry the load it is lighter. Grief shared is easier to bear.

I have been given another gift. In the three years since Ruth left, I have never dreamed about her except once. It was a strange dream, yet a beautiful one. In it I saw nothing but a dark cloud overshadowing me, and through it I heard Ruth's clear soprano singing a hymn. I awakened still hearing her beautiful voice in my mind. To me it was God telling me that my Ruthie was happy with Him.

So what is my answer to Satan's challenge when he dares God to *"put forth thine hand now and touch all that [they] hath, and [they] will curse thee to thy face?"* (Job 1:11).

"I still love You, Lord," I cry to Him, "my God and my Savior."

This Is My Story This Is My Song

Chapter Sixteen

A Golden Mirror and a Golden Cross

It was a very special moment as Mike and I stood looking over the empty ballroom of the Top of the Bellevue Hotel that September 28, 1991. We would be marking our golden wedding anniversary that evening. But we did not know we'd be celebrating another special event that night as we looked over the sea of tables covered with gold cloths stretching before us. On top of them, "bouquets" of tiny gold lights winked. In another hour some five hundred guests would stream into the ballroom.

But now was a very special time for us. Just the two of us standing alone reminded me of that moment more than fifty years ago when we sat on a park bench overlooking the sun-dappled Schuykill river not far from this hotel. That was when the man now at my side proposed to me.

"Seems like only yesterday," he murmured, squeezing my hand.

"Yes," I sighed, "and you're just as handsome as ever."

"Even though that's not true, thank you anyway, Fran," he laughed.

We strolled back to the foyer where my white satin wedding gown was displayed along with our wedding picture. Mike poked me. "Think you can still fit into it?"

I poked him back. "Just as well as you could fit into that rented tuxedo."

He reached out and touched a lily petal on the replica of my wedding bouquet next to the gown. "Bet we could buy twenty of the original with what *this* one cost," he said.

"And you could buy a new car then for a thousand dollars," I countered.

"Yes," he admitted, "times sure have changed." He gave me a quick hug. "But you're just as sweet as ever."

As we walked down to the reception room where we'd meet our guests, he continued, "Fran, I don't know what I would have done without you…sticking with me through thick and thin, raising the kids, helping me get the business going when everybody said I was crazy for starting it."

As we walked along arm in arm, I thought, *What had made the difference?* There were so many times he or I could have walked out of our relationship in anger or disappointment. According to recent statistics half of all marriages fail. Why did ours succeed? We still had our arguments. In fact, our most recent one was about the program for this very celebration. But we came to an agreement. One thing Mike and I have both learned: It doesn't pay to have "the last word." The last word kills marriages. We also learned to never "let the sun go down on your anger" (Eph. 4:26, RSV).

But there is more than that to a good marriage—it is commitment, unselfishly giving of yourselves to the other, come what may. Too many people today, it seems, put self-gratification first. If everything doesn't go their way, they automatically think of divorce. In our day it was a sin even to say the word. And so it was this evening, obedient to that vow we made before God to love, honor and obey, for better or worse, for richer or poorer, in sickness and in health, we were happily celebrating our fiftieth year.

I'm sure I'll be blasted by the women's lib group, but I think a wife has a God-given power to keep a marriage together. Somehow a wife knows how to bend, how to understand her husband, who can sometimes act like a little boy. In so doing she becomes the steel in the strength of a marriage. And, to me, that's *real* women's liberation.

As I glanced at the man walking alongside me, I thanked God for him. He had certainly fulfilled the admonition of the apostle Paul, who told us in 2 Corinthians 5:15 (TLB): *"He died for all so that all who live...might live no longer for themselves, to please themselves, but to spend their lives pleasing Christ who died and rose again for them."*

I could see it in the faces of the guests who came up to congratulate us. I thought of the churches Mike helped build around the world, his giving to the Lord as founding regent of Oral Roberts University, his funding the Media Center for the Assemblies of God headquarters in Springfield, Missouri, to further the Word of Christ around the world. This is what makes a happy man, giving.

As the festivities of the evening commenced with good food, music and a large-screen projection of family highlights through the years, I thought of other loved ones not with us. My mother, who would have been so proud to see this day; my father, who had once worked in this very room as a waiter many years ago; Mike's parents; and, of course, Ruth. As our friend Judge Joseph Bruno said in his talk, "I'm sure she's happy and smiling down at us."

She would have been especially happy to see what her and her brother's children did that night. There's an old saying that the crown of one's later years is grandchildren. And ours crowned us with glory that night.

All of them assembled on the stage and sang to us a beautiful song, titled simply "Thank You." Michael III played the electric bass, Patricia played the piano, Roger played the drums, Christin and Ryan sang, and Eric announced. In it they expressed their appreciation for "all the wonderful things you've done." When I looked at Mike, I saw tears in his eyes; they were also in mine. I knew that he was celebrating the fact that all of our children and grandchildren were saved and serving the Lord.

As I gazed on each grandchild, memories filled my heart. There was Michael III, to whom I was now sending my home-cooked spaghetti sauce so he could treat his fellow students at the university, just as I had done for his father. Only now I sent it by Federal Express. Whether he'll work at Cardone Industries, I don't know. He works there part-time now and attends meetings. Just the other day he said something very insightful about a factory operation; I turned to him and asked, "Michael, how come you know so much?"

His quiet answer was, "I listen."

There was beautiful little Christin; Ryan, our miracle grandchild; Patricia, who is following in her mother's footsteps by playing the piano; Eric, who calls me every day and makes me feel loved; and Roger, who when I asked what he thought of certain evangelists who had gone astray, answered wisely, "Grandma, they weren't living close to the Lord."

And it was Roger who came up with the stunning surprise of the evening. His wife, Miriam, had just given birth. Months before I had told her in jest that "I want that baby to be born on our anniversary." Such timing seemed an impossibility, and I forgot it.

But God must have wanted to add His special touch to our night. For, lo and behold, as we celebrated that evening, a news flash came from Roger at Holy Redeemer Hospital that our first great-grandchild, Jeffrey, had been born! The ballroom broke into applause. Roger raced to the hotel from the hospital with a videotape just taken of mother and child which was projected on the giant screen for all to enjoy.

Mike and I couldn't have had a more exciting anniversary gift.

Other great-grandchildren have followed since then.

Eric and Lisa's first child, David, was born in June 1992, and Roger's second, a girl, came in March 1993.

All our married grandchildren have wonderful spouses. For as I have written previously, their parents had taken a cue from us and prayed for their children's future mates. Not only did they pray, but they began helping them understand early in life how important it was for them to find someone who really shared their faith. To me that's half the battle. One other important point which I'd like to make right now: A pastor I know, when counseling couples before marriage, always asks if they find it easy to talk together. For example, if the television breaks down and they find themselves with nothing to do, can they have a good conversation? I know this is vital for I have heard it said that a good marriage is one long conversation. Mike and I can attest to that.

Yes, we all are still one big family and now we all are involved in our new church, The Christian Life Center.

So much a part of us remains with Calvary Temple, where our children were schooled and where I played the organ for so long. In fact, a part of me will never leave, and that's the three giant-sized oil paintings I created with a palette knife that hang on the church walls. *The Lord Is My Shepherd* portrays Christ with His sheep, *The Harvest Is Great and the Laborers Are Few* shows men harvesting wheat (both of these measure three and one-half feet square), and the third is a painting of Calvary Temple (which measures over five feet square).

However, the Lord had given Mike and me a vision

that He wanted another church started close to where we live in northern Philadelphia.

After much prayer, we began in 1990 with a small group of us meeting in Michael and Jacquie's house. I must admit it was with much fear and trembling. *Oh, only a handful of people,* I worried. *What are we doing?* And then it was as if the Lord spoke to me: *Remember, I started with just twelve people.*

By the second month we had grown to where we rented a banquet hall in a shopping center in north of Huntington Valley, and called our church The Christian Life Center. Our first Pastor, Rev. Greg Cox led our fledgling congregation. We learned that if you obey God and take that step of faith, something wonderful happens.

For it is now very clear what God meant when He said, *"Build my church here."* There were many people who *were* searching for spiritual nourishment but didn't know where to find it until they came to The Christian Life Center. They included business executives, doctors, lawyers, teachers and many others whom some call the "up-and-outers."

When you link yourself closely with God, you find yourself being carried to surprising new heights. And that's what happened to our church. It soon became evident we were bursting the seams of the banquet hall, and we had to find new space.

Where and what? This was the problem. There were no halls big enough to accommodate our growing congregation. And we did not have the funds to build a new building from scratch. You can be sure a lot of prayer ascended to heaven from all around Huntington

Valley.

They say man's extremity is God's opportunity. A small group of Christians in nearby Bensalem had purchased six acres on which they hoped to build a church. However, after getting only four walls erected, they ran out of money. Hearing of our need, they approached us wondering if we could join together and finish God's house.

God couldn't have answered our prayers any better. Of course we could, and the new church was completed. Brethen, David Cawston, a gifted preacher had become our Pastor. It was dedicated in memory of our daughter, Ruth, on May 8, 1993 by Dr. James Kennedy of Coral Ridge Presbyterian Church in Florida, and Dr. Joseph R. Flower of the Assemblies of God headquarters.

I find it so interesting how, if a family makes their church the central focus of their lives, the oncoming generation seems to grow into it naturally. All our grandchildren tithe, and I get a special kick out of Eric, who is so keen on the new church that when it was under construction you could often find him on the site overseeing the work. I joked to him about being its "construction foreman."

The Lord is already working through The Christian Life Center, which now serves over eight hundred people. A man doing some repair work on our house was about the furthest person you could think of from being a Christian. Rough and tough, he was very much the macho man. Of course, working around Mike and me, he couldn't help overhear us talking. We were discussing our new church a lot, along with what the Lord has done in our lives. He may have heard me talk about a problem we faced in Florida. We had two small houses situated next to each other on a small lot that we wanted to sell. However due to the housing glut on the market, it seemed an impossibility. It would also be difficult to find someone in need of two houses together like that.

"Mike, I'm continually praying about it," I remember telling my husband. "And I believe the Lord is going to bring us a buyer. So I'm putting it in His hands completely. Somewhere out there is a person who really needs two houses like that, and the Lord will bring us together."

"It will take a miracle," said Mike, "but I'll pray with you."

The miracle happened. A couple with two sisters were desperately seeking such a place, and they bought it. The couple moved into the bigger house, and the two sisters were very happy in the guest house.

Afterward, I related the outcome of our prayers to a group of people. One woman scoffed, "You can't tell me God is interested in little things like selling houses."

When I told Mike about it over lunch, he smiled, "Well, if the Lord has His eye on the sparrow and counts the hairs of our head, as we're told in the Bible, I'm sure He's interested in helping people find the right place to live."

"It's just what our pastor at church was saying last Sunday," he added, "if one follows the principles of the Bible, things will always work out to His glory."

The following Sunday we got the surprise of our life. When we walked into church, who should be sitting in a front row but none other than our macho repairman!

This is the kind of witnessing Mike and I like to do—letting others see God working in our lives. A poem I read in Guideposts magazine some time ago puts our feelings into words:

The Gospel According to You

The most beautiful story given to man
Was written long ago
By Matthew, Mark, Luke and John
Of Christ and His mission below.

And you write a gospel, a chapter a day,
By your deeds, whether faithless or true;
When others read it, what will they think
Of the gospel according to you?

It's a wonderful story, the gospel of love,
As it shines with Christ's life divine.
Oh, that its truth might be told again
In the story of your life and mine.

You are writing each day a letter to men;
Take care that the writing is true.
It's the only gospel some people may read,
That gospel according to you.

—Wallace E. Norwood

Recently I saw this principle at work in a restaurant where we were having dinner with other family members. A guitar player was entertaining. When he came to our table, I asked if he could play "Amazing Grace." He wasn't that sure, so I said, "If I sing it, can you follow me?"

"Sure," he said, and we all started singing, *"Amazing grace! How sweet the sound that saved a wretch like me! I once was lost but now am found. Was blind but now I see...."* He strummed along with us, and we sang some more gospel songs.

"Say," he said, "I *like* your songs." Mike started talking with him, asking about his family and his hopes for the future. The musician seemed touched that someone was taking an interest in him. Usually no one seems to give a strolling musician a second thought except to toss him a dollar. Soon the two were talking about Jesus, and Mike invited him to our house. "Bring your wife and your guitar," he said.

He was over the next day along with some others we had invited. We were having a good visit when suddenly the guitar player stood up and said, "I want to say something."

The room became silent as he stood there looking embarrassed. It was obvious he was struggling over what he wanted to say. Finally, taking a quick look at Mike and wiping his brow, he said, "I've been watching Mr. Cardone, how he acts and lives. If he can live like that, I want to do so too. And I think I can with Jesus' help."

He stopped and wiped his eyes. Then, voice choked with emotion, he continued: "I have lived a bad life. Yesterday...yesterday," he stopped and looked at his wife, who was sitting open-mouthed. "Yesterday I had decided to get a divorce. Today, before we came here, I told my wife I wasn't going to ask for one.

"Why?" He pointed to my husband. "If a man like Mr. Cardone can live the way he does, I want to live that way too, and I know I can with the help of Jesus."

His wife broke into tears, and I think everybody else was crying too. A pastor was visiting; he prayed for the guitar player and his wife. We all joined in.

It's folks finding the Lord, like the guitar player and the macho man who joined our church, that makes life worth living for us today. I don't know how much time we have left; only the Lord knows. Mike, as of this writing, is seventy-seven, and I prepare healthy foods for him—he likes vegetables and pasta, particularly broccoli and macaroni, avoiding steaks and other rich meats. He's supposed to be semi-retired, but he still goes like a house on fire.

It seemed all the good he had accomplished in his work came together when he was elected into the international Automotive Hall of Fame in 1994. This 55-year-old prestigious organization honors men and women who have made distinguished contributions to the automotive industry. He was especially proud to be inducted along with fellow honoree, Lee Iacocca, former chairman of the Chrysler Corporation. Other men inducted into the Hall of Fame include Henry Ford, David Buick, Harvey Firestone and Louis Chevrolet. Mike had been previously recognized by the Hall of Fame in 1984 when he was awarded a Distinguished Service Citation for his foresight in establishing a remanufacturing business.

Our son, Michael Jr., was also honored by the Hall of Fame in 1982 when he was presented an award for Young Leadership and Excellence.

I am so proud of them.

As Psalm 1:2 says: "...his delight is in the law of the Lord, and on his law he meditates day and night" (RSV).

Me? Recently the doctors found another tumor that appeared to be malignant. All of us prayed, including a lot of people around the country, and it disappeared. As one of my grandchildren said: "Grandma, you've got nine lives, just like a cat."

The other afternoon I accompanied Mike to our manufacturing plant offices to pick up some papers. As I waited in the car, I looked at the buildings extending into the distance, the big tractor trailers bearing the name *Cardone Industries,* and I marveled, thinking back to how Mike and I started remanufacturing windshield wiper motors in a little storefront shop a quarter of a century ago.

When Mike came back to the car, I was about to say, "Isn't it wonderful what we have accomplished?" But I caught myself. It wasn't us, it was God. Without Him nothing would have happened. God has given us His Holy Spirit to *use* us, to perform His work *through* our abilities. The Holy Spirit is not ours to use; it is for Him to use us.

With that in mind, I asked Mike to drive past the new Christian Life Center. It was evening when we arrived at the church. The sun was setting behind the building, and all was quiet. We got out of the car and slowly walked around it, then stopped, looking at its tower. I took Mike's hand. "It's a lot different from the old *Chiesa Italiano Pentecostale,*" I murmured.

He squeezed my hand and said, "Yes, but it's quite the same too."

I looked up at the golden cross on its tower and knew what he meant.

THE KEYS TO SUCCESS
AND HAPPINESS

Would you like the same help that guided Frances Cardone in her life? It's your's for the asking. All you have to do is:

• Admit that you are a sinner and need to be saved. "For all have sinned, and come short of the glory of God" (Romans 3:23). When we frankly admit this, we've taken the first step.

• Believe Jesus has provided your salvation. "For God so loved the wold, that he gave his only begotten Son, that whosoever believeth in him should not perish, but have everlasting life" (John 3:16). Jesus said, "I am the way, the truth, and the life: no man cometh unto the Father, but by me" (John 14:6).

- Repent of your sin by turning away from it. "Repent ye therefore, and be converted, that your sins may be blotted out..." (Acts 3:19).

- Accept God's forgiveness. "If we confess our sins, he is faithful and just to forgive us our sins, and to cleanse us from all unrighteousness" (1 John 1:9).

- Confess Say aloud what you believe. "If thou shalt confess with thy mouth the Lord Jesus, and shalt believe in thine heart that God hath raised him from the dead, thou shalt be saved" (Romans 10:9).

With Jesus in your heart, you are no longer a slave to worry, fear, and depression. If you let God take over, life will become new and exciting. Jesus said, "...I am come that they might have life, and that they might have it more abundantly" (John 10:10). Not only will your life be filled with joy, peace, and happiness, you will also receive the assurance of eternal life through Christ! Jesus said, "...He that heareth my word and believeth on him that sent me, hath everlasting life, and shall not come into condemnation; but is passed from death unto life" (John 5:24).

Your can receive salvation now by praying this prayer out loud:

Dear God, Your Word shows that I have sinned and need to be saved by Jesus Christ. I repent of my sin and turn to Your, Jesus. I believe that You died, were resurrected, and now live. I commit my life to You. Be my Lord and make me a child of God. Father I thank You for my salvation in Jesus' name. Amen.

Rejoice in your new life—a life of "joy unspeakable and full of glory."

If you would like to know more about how God can guide you, write to:

Frances Cardone
P.O. Box 622
Huntingdon Valley, PA 19006

This Is My Story This Is My Song